IMMIGRATION

OPPOSING VIEWPOINTS®

Mary E. Williams, *Book Editor*

Daniel Leone, *President*
Bonnie Szumski, *Publisher*
Scott Barbour, *Managing Editor*
Helen Cothran, *Senior Editor*

OPPOSING
VIEWPOINTS®
SERIES

GREENHAVEN
PRESS®

THOMSON

GALE

San Diego • Detroit • New York • San Francisco • Cleveland
New Haven, Conn. • Waterville, Maine • London • Munich

THOMSON
✳ ™
GALE

© 2004 by Greenhaven Press. Greenhaven Press is an imprint of The Gale Group, Inc., a division of Thomson Learning, Inc.

Greenhaven® and Thomson Learning™ are trademarks used herein under license.

For more information, contact
Greenhaven Press
27500 Drake Rd.
Farmington Hills, MI 48331-3535
Or you can visit our Internet site at http://www.gale.com

Cover credit: Photodisc

LIBRARY OF CONGRESS CATALOGING-IN-PUBLICATION DATA
Immigration : opposing viewpoints / Mary E. Williams, book editor.
    p. cm. — (Opposing viewpoints series)
Includes bibliographical references and index.
ISBN 0-7377-1692-4 (pbk. : alk. paper) —
ISBN 0-7377-1691-6 (lib. bdg. : alk. paper)
    1. Immigrants—Government policy—United States. 2. United States—
Emigration and immigration—Government policy. I. Williams, Mary E., 1960– .
II. Opposing viewpoints series (Unnumbered)
JV6483.I5533 2004
325.73—dc21   2003048320

Printed in the United States of America

"Congress shall make no law...abridging the freedom of speech, or of the press."

First Amendment to the U.S. Constitution

The basic foundation of our democracy is the First Amendment guarantee of freedom of expression. The Opposing Viewpoints Series is dedicated to the concept of this basic freedom and the idea that it is more important to practice it than to enshrine it.

Contents

Why Consider Opposing Viewpoints?

"The only way in which a human being can make some approach to knowing the whole of a subject is by hearing what can be said about it by persons of every variety of opinion and studying all modes in which it can be looked at by every character of mind. No wise man ever acquired his wisdom in any mode but this."

John Stuart Mill

In our media-intensive culture it is not difficult to find differing opinions. Thousands of newspapers and magazines and dozens of radio and television talk shows resound with differing points of view. The difficulty lies in deciding which opinion to agree with and which "experts" seem the most credible. The more inundated we become with differing opinions and claims, the more essential it is to hone critical reading and thinking skills to evaluate these ideas. Opposing Viewpoints books address this problem directly by presenting stimulating debates that can be used to enhance and teach these skills. The varied opinions contained in each book examine many different aspects of a single issue. While examining these conveniently edited opposing views, readers can develop critical thinking skills such as the ability to compare and contrast authors' credibility, facts, argumentation styles, use of persuasive techniques, and other stylistic tools. In short, the Opposing Viewpoints Series is an ideal way to attain the higher-level thinking and reading skills so essential in a culture of diverse and contradictory opinions.

In addition to providing a tool for critical thinking, Opposing Viewpoints books challenge readers to question their own strongly held opinions and assumptions. Most people form their opinions on the basis of upbringing, peer pressure, and personal, cultural, or professional bias. By reading carefully balanced opposing views, readers must directly confront new ideas as well as the opinions of those with whom they disagree. This is not to simplistically argue that everyone who reads opposing views will—or should—change his or her opinion. Instead, the series enhances readers' understanding of their own views by encouraging confrontation with opposing ideas. Careful examination of others' views can lead to the readers' understanding of the logical inconsistencies in their own opinions, perspective on why they hold an opinion, and the consideration of the possibility that their opinion requires further evaluation.

Evaluating Other Opinions

To ensure that this type of examination occurs, Opposing Viewpoints books present all types of opinions. Prominent spokespeople on different sides of each issue as well as well-known professionals from many disciplines challenge the reader. An additional goal of the series is to provide a forum for other, less known, or even unpopular viewpoints. The opinion of an ordinary person who has had to make the decision to cut off life support from a terminally ill relative, for example, may be just as valuable and provide just as much insight as a medical ethicist's professional opinion. The editors have two additional purposes in including these less known views. One, the editors encourage readers to respect others' opinions—even when not enhanced by professional credibility. It is only by reading or listening to and objectively evaluating others' ideas that one can determine whether they are worthy of consideration. Two, the inclusion of such viewpoints encourages the important critical thinking skill of objectively evaluating an author's credentials and bias. This evaluation will illuminate an author's reasons for taking a particular stance on an issue and will aid in readers' evaluation of the author's ideas.

It is our hope that these books will give readers a deeper understanding of the issues debated and an appreciation of the complexity of even seemingly simple issues when good and honest people disagree. This awareness is particularly important in a democratic society such as ours in which people enter into public debate to determine the common good. Those with whom one disagrees should not be regarded as enemies but rather as people whose views deserve careful examination and may shed light on one's own.

Thomas Jefferson once said that "difference of opinion leads to inquiry, and inquiry to truth." Jefferson, a broadly educated man, argued that "if a nation expects to be ignorant and free . . . it expects what never was and never will be." As individuals and as a nation, it is imperative that we consider the opinions of others and examine them with skill and discernment. The Opposing Viewpoints Series is intended to help readers achieve this goal.

David L. Bender and Bruno Leone,
Founders

Greenhaven Press anthologies primarily consist of previously published material taken from a variety of sources, including periodicals, books, scholarly journals, newspapers, government documents, and position papers from private and public organizations. These original sources are often edited for length and to ensure their accessibility for a young adult audience. The anthology editors also change the original titles of these works in order to clearly present the main thesis of each viewpoint and to explicitly indicate the opinion presented in the viewpoint. These alterations are made in consideration of both the reading and comprehension levels of a young adult audience. Every effort is made to ensure that Greenhaven Press accurately reflects the original intent of the authors included in this anthology.

Introduction

"Today, the annual tidal wave of over a million immigrants . . . is endangering our American way of life."

                      —*Americans for Immigration Control*

"Immigration is not undermining the American experiment; it is an integral part of it."

                      —*Daniel T. Griswold*

Between 1790 and 1920 the population of the United States grew from 4 million to 106 million. About 1 million new immigrants—most of them European—had arrived each year, and by the 1920 census, the foreign-born comprised more than 13 percent of the U.S. population. Responding to public anxieties about this large influx of newcomers, Congress passed the Quota Act in 1921, which set a cap of 360,000 new immigrants per year. This act also established a national-origins preference that favored immigrants from England, Scandinavia, Germany, and France over those from southern Europe, Asia, and Africa. Coupled with the impact of the Depression and World War II, these regulations dramatically reduced immigration to the United States. Between 1930 and 1950 only 4 million newcomers became American citizens—less than half the number of immigrants that had arrived during the first decade of the twentieth century.

In the 1960s significant policy revisions again changed the makeup and number of immigrants coming to the United States. Prompted by the successes of the civil rights movement, Congress chose to end racially restrictive immigration quotas by passing the Immigration and Nationality Act of 1965. This act, which took effect in 1968, set an annual immigration cap of 290,000—170,000 from the Eastern Hemisphere and 120,000 from the Western Hemisphere. In addition, this new law established a "family preference" rule, which granted favor to the close relatives of immigrants already living in the United States. In effect, relatives of immigrants who were U.S. citizens were exempt from the quota system. During the mid-1960s,

Latin American and Asian countries still had a relatively low proportion of visas available to immigrants, but due to the family preference system, it was not long before these countries contributed a substantial portion of America's new immigrants. By 1990, 44 percent of America's legal immigrants were from Latin America and the Caribbean, and 36 percent came from Asia. Less than 15 percent were from Europe.

The new quota system and family preference policy were not the only factors affecting the numbers and demographics of U.S. immigrants. Illegal immigration of migrant workers increased dramatically after the 1965 Immigration Act cancelled the Bracero program, which since the 1940s had allowed foreigners—mostly Mexicans—to take temporary agricultural jobs in California and Texas. In one of its first serious attempts to control illegal immigration, Congress passed the Immigration Reform and Control Act (IRCA) in 1986. The act had two parts: It provided amnesty to illegal immigrants who could prove they met certain requirements for living and working in the United States, and it sanctioned employers for hiring undocumented workers. Most analysts agree, however, that the IRCA had little effect in reducing illegal immigration. According to the U.S. Immigration and Naturalization Service, about 200,000 to 300,000 illegal immigrants enter the United States annually.

Not only did restrictions on illegal immigration fail to significantly reduce the total number of immigrants entering the country, but new policies led to overall increases. Higher immigration caps that took effect in 1990 now allow 700,000 to one million legal immigrants into America each year. Out of a current total U.S. population of 284 million, immigrants comprise 10 percent of American residents— 28.4 million. By the year 2050 the U.S. population is projected to increase to 400 million, with immigrants contributing to two-thirds of that growth.

For many Americans, such a large number of newcomers—and the prospect of millions more—is unsettling. Some experts are concerned that the accelerated population growth resulting from immigration could overtax the country's municipal, natural, and economic resources. Sociologist Christopher Jencks, for example, maintains that cities will become grossly overcrowded, resulting in gridlocked traffic, suburban sprawl, increased pollution, and dwindling power and water supplies. A similar premise—that continued immigration means fewer or lower-quality resources for current residents—underlies economic arguments for immigration restrictions. For instance, some economists contend that because immigrants are often poor and uneducated, they take jobs that otherwise would have gone to low-skilled native-born workers. And since newcomers are willing to work for low pay, they depress wages across the nation. As Federation for American Immigration Reform director Dan Stein argues, "All we're doing is importing a huge pool of cheap labor, which helps employers but keeps wages low for Americans." In addition, critics maintain, poverty rates are high among new immigrants, so they make disproportionate use of welfare and other social services. This places even more economic burdens on ordinary Americans, who must support welfare by paying taxes.

Still other analysts fear that a steady stream of immigrants could undermine the nation's ability to absorb and integrate recent arrivals into American society. Large blocs of unassimilated immigrants, they claim, could divide the nation along ethnic lines. The fact that most of today's immigrants are from Latin America or Asia is particularly troublesome for commentators like Patrick Buchanan, who contends that too many of these newcomers have "no desire to learn English or become citizens." *National Review* editor John O'Sullivan agrees, arguing that immigration must be restricted to give schools and other institutions time to teach current immigrants English and American values. "In order to work together effectively we must maximize our common cultural sympathies," O'Sullivan asserts. "If every ethnic group retains its own cultural sympathies, it will be hard for us to work together as one people."

Immigration supporters, however, believe that most of the economic and cultural concerns voiced by restrictionists are unfounded. For example, many experts refute the assertion that foreign-born workers take jobs from Americans. They point out that cities with the largest immigrant populations have always had faster economic growth and lower unemployment than cities that do not draw immigrants. Moreover, highly skilled immigrants as well as uneducated newcomers are motivated, hardworking people who close gaps in the U.S. job market. Maintains Daniel Griswold of the Cato Institute, "Immigrants tend to fill jobs that Americans cannot or will not fill, mostly at the high and low ends of the skill spectrum. Immigrants are disproportionately represented in such high-skilled fields as medicine, physics and computer science, but also in lower-skilled sectors such as hotels and restaurants, domestic service, construction and light manufacturing." Immigrants also start more small businesses than native-born Americans do, which creates employment opportunities that help to lessen the effects of economic recessions, analysts point out.

Immigration proponents also discount restrictionists' concerns about the assimilation of large numbers of newcomers. The vast majority of immigrants want very much to become American citizens, argues immigration expert Bronwyn Lance. "Very few would run the gauntlet to get here unless they wanted to become part of this country," Lance points out. Furthermore, as author Tamar Jacoby maintains, it is simply untrue that immigrants refuse to learn English: "Many more than in previous eras come with a working knowledge of the language—it is hard to avoid in the world today." Griswold, Lance, Jacoby, and other experts contend that new immigrants will likely follow in the footsteps of their predecessors, who worked hard to become a part of American society while retaining ties to their cultural heritage.

Since its founding in 1776, the United States has been a nation of immigrants; the image of America welcoming the huddled masses to its shores is an integral part of how Americans view themselves and their country. *Immigration: Opposing Viewpoints* examines the issues pertaining to legal and illegal immigration in the following chapters: Historical Debate: Should Immigration Be Restricted? Is Immigration a Serious Problem? How Should the United States Address Illegal Immigration? How Should U.S. Immigration Policy Be Reformed? The authors in this anthology explore the continuing ambivalence about immigration and America's vision of itself as the land of freedom and opportunity.

CHAPTER 1

Historical Debate: Should Immigration Be Restricted?

Chapter Preface

The debate over immigration is as old as the United States itself. "Despite the fact that almost all of us are immigrants or descendants of immigrants," writes immigration scholar George J. Borjas, "American history is characterized by a never-ending debate over when to pull the ladder in." Each wave of new immigrants—Irish in the 1840s, Chinese in the 1870s, Italians at the turn of the twentieth century, Cubans in the 1960s, Southeast Asians in the 1970s, and others—has sparked controversy among Americans whose immigrant forebears arrived earlier.

Many of the historical complaints about immigration are similar to those voiced today. The People's Party platform of 1882 proclaimed, "We condemn . . . the present system, which opens up our ports to the pauper and criminal classes of the world, and crowds out our wage earners." Borjas comments, "It seems that little has changed in the past hundred years. Today the same accusations are hurled at illegal aliens, at boat people originating in Southeast Asia and Cuba, and at other unskilled immigrants."

A prevalent concern throughout the historical immigration debate is race and ethnicity. Many people believed that the latest immigrants to arrive in the United States were racially inferior to those who dominated previous immigration waves. Around the turn of the twentieth century, for example, Francis Walker, president of the Massachusetts Institute of Technology, described the incoming Italians, Greeks, Poles, and Russians as "beaten men from beaten races, representing the worst failures in the struggle for existence." Racism also played a major role in the immigration laws passed in the 1920s. These laws severely limited immigration from Asia, Latin America, and southern and eastern Europe. Their passage and eventual repeal in 1965 are major turning points in the history of U.S. immigration. Another major turning point—the terrorist attacks of September 11, 2001—raised concerns about immigrants from Arab, south Asian, and Muslim nations as U.S. policy makers considered how to respond to the threat of future terrorism.

Examining past debates on immigration can shed light on

present-day controversies. The viewpoints in this chapter present arguments on immigration at three different periods in American history: the middle nineteenth century and the early twentieth century—during great waves of European immigration—and the latter twentieth century, just before racially restrictive immigration quotas were ended.

> "The emigration of foreigners to this country is not only defensible on grounds of abstract justice . . . [but] it has been in various ways highly beneficial to this country."

America Should Welcome Immigration (1845)

Thomas L. Nichols

Thomas L. Nichols (1815–1901) was a doctor, dietician, social historian, and journalist. In the following viewpoint, written in 1845, he criticizes movements in the United States to restrict immigration. He argues that prejudices against immigrants are unfounded and that immigration has been beneficial to the United States.

As you read, consider the following questions:
1. What racial beliefs does Nichols express concerning immigration?
2. How does the author characterize American immigrants?
3. According to Nichols, what is the worst thing that can be said about immigrants?

Thomas L. Nichols, "Lecture on Immigration and the Rights of Naturalization," *Historical Aspects of the Immigration Problem*, edited by Edith Abbott. New York: Arno Press, 1969.

The questions connected with emigration from Europe to America are interesting to both the old world and the new—are of importance to the present and future generations. They have more consequence than a charter or a state election; they involve the destinies of millions; they are connected with the progress of civilization, the rights of man, and providence of God!

Examining Prejudices

I have examined this subject the more carefully, and speak upon it the more earnestly, because I have been to some extent, in former years, a partaker of the prejudices I have since learned to pity. A native of New England and a descendant of the puritans, I early imbibed, and to some extent promulgated, opinions of which reflection and experience have made me ashamed. . . .

Believing that the principles and practices of Native Americanism are wrong in themselves, and are doing wrong to those who are the objects of their persecution, justice and humanity require that their fallacy should be exposed, and their iniquity condemned. It may be unfortunate that the cause of the oppressed and persecuted, in opinion if not in action, has not fallen into other hands; yet, let me trust that the truth, even in mine, will prove mighty, prevailing from its own inherent power!

The right of man to emigrate from one country to another, is one which belongs to him by his own constitution and by every principle of justice. It is one which no law can alter, and no authority destroy. "Life, liberty, and the pursuit of happiness" are set down, in our Declaration of Independence, as among the self-evident, unalienable rights of man. If I have a right to live, I have also a right to what will support existence—food, clothing, and shelter. If then the country in which I reside, from a superabundant population, or any other cause, does not afford me these, my right to go from it to some other is self-evident and unquestionable. The *right to live*, then, supposes the right of emigration. . . .

The emigration of foreigners to this country is not only defensible on grounds of abstract justice—what we have no possible right to prevent, but . . . it has been in various ways highly beneficial to this country.

Emigration first peopled this hemisphere with civilized men. The first settlers of this continent had the same right to come here that belongs to the emigrant of yesterday—no better and no other. They came to improve their condition, to escape from oppression, to enjoy freedom—for the same, or similar, reasons as now prevail. And so far as they violated no private rights, so long as they obtained their lands by fair purchase, or took possession of those which were unclaimed and uncultivated, the highly respectable natives whom the first settlers found here had no right to make any objections. The peopling of this continent with civilized men, the cultivation of the earth, the various processes of productive labor, for the happiness of man, all tend to "the greatest good of the greatest number," and carry out the evident design of Nature or Providence in the formation of the earth and its inhabitants.

Let Them Come

The poor flock to our shores to escape from a state of penury, which cannot be relieved by toil in their own native land. The man of enterprise comes, to avail himself of the advantages afforded by a wider and more varied field for the exercise of his industry and talents; and the oppressed of every land, thirsting for deliverance from the paralyzing effects of unjust institutions, come to enjoy the blessings of a government which secures life, liberty, and the pursuit of happiness to all its constituents. Let them come. They will convert our waste lands into fruitful fields, vineyards, and gardens; construct works of public improvement; build up and establish manufactures; and open our rich mines of coal, of iron, of lead, and of copper. And more than all, they will be the means of augmenting our commerce, and aiding us in extending the influence of our political, social, and religious institutions throughout the earth.

Western Journal, vol. 6, 1851.

Emigration from various countries in Europe to America, producing a mixture of races, has had, and is still having, the most important influence upon the destinies of the human race. It is a principle, laid down by every physiologist, and proved by abundant observation, that man, like other animals, is improved and brought to its highest perfection by an intermingling of the blood and qualities of various races. That nations and families deteriorate from an opposite course has been observed in all ages. The great physiological reason why Americans are superior to other nations in freedom, intelligence, and enterprise, is because that they are the offspring of the greatest intermingling of races. The mingled blood of England has given her predominance over several nations of Europe in these very qualities, and a newer infusion, with favorable circumstances of climate, position, and institutions, has rendered Americans still superior. The Yankees of New England would never have shown those qualities for which they have been distinguished in war and peace throughout the world had there not been mingled with the puritan English, the calculating Scotch, the warm hearted Irish, the gay and chivalric French, the steady persevering Dutch, and the transcendental Germans, for all these nations contributed to make up the New England character, before the Revolution, and ever since to influence that of the whole American people.

It is not too much to assert that in the order of Providence this vast and fertile continent was reserved for this great destiny; to be the scene of this mingling of the finest European races, and consequently of the highest condition of human intelligence, freedom, and happiness; for I look upon this mixture of the blood and qualities of various nations, and its continual infusion, as absolutely requisite to the perfection of humanity. . . . Continual emigration, and a constant mixing of the blood of different races, is highly conducive to physical and mental superiority.

Economic Benefits

This country has been continually benefited by the immense amount of capital brought hither by emigrants. There are very few who arrive upon our shores without some little store of wealth, the hoard of years of industry. Small as these means may be in each case, they amount to millions in the aggregate, and every dollar is so much added to the wealth of the country, to be reckoned at compound interest from the time of its arrival, nor are these sums like our European loans, which we must pay back, both principal and interest.

Within a few years, especially, and more or less at all periods, men of great wealth have been among the emigrants driven from Europe, by religious oppression or political revolutions. Vast sums have also fallen to emigrants and their descendants by inheritance, for every few days we read in the papers of some poor foreigner, or descendant of foreigners, as are we all, becoming the heir of a princely fortune, which in most cases, is added to the wealth of his adopted country. Besides this, capital naturally follows labor, and it flows upon this country in a constant current, by the laws of trade.

Receive Them as Friends

Let us by no means join in the popular outcry against foreigners coming to our country, and partaking of its privileges. They will come, whether we will or no; and is it wise to meet them with inhospitality, and thus turn their hearts against us? Let us rather receive them as friends, and give them welcome to our country. Let us rather say, "The harvest before us is indeed great, and the laborers are few: come, go with us, and we will do thee good." Our hills, and valleys, and rivers, stretch from ocean to ocean, belting the entire continent of the New World; and over this rich and boundless domain, Providence has poured the atmosphere of liberty. Let these poor sufferers come and breathe it freely. Let our country be the asylum of the oppressed of all lands. Let those who come bent down with the weight of European tithes and taxation, here throw off the load, and stand erect in freedom.

Samuel Griswold Goodrich, *Ireland and the Irish*, 1841.

But it is not money alone that adds to the wealth of a country but every day's productive labor is to be added to its accumulating capital. Every house built, every canal dug, every railroad graded, has added so much to the actual wealth of society; and who have built more houses, dug more canals, or graded more railroads, than the hardy Irishmen? I hardly know how our great national works could have been carried on without them then; while every pair of sturdy arms has added to our national wealth, every hungry mouth has been a home market for our agriculture, and every broad shoulder has been clothed with our manufactures.

From the very nature of the case, America gets from Europe the most valuable of her population. Generally, those who come here are the very ones whom a sensible man would select. Those who are attached to monarchical and aristocratic institutions stay at home where they can enjoy them. Those who lack energy and enterprise can never make up their minds to leave their native land. It is the strong minded, the brave hearted, the free and self-respecting, the enterprising and the intelligent, who break away from all the ties of country and of home, and brave the dangers of the ocean, in search of liberty and independence, for themselves and for their children, on a distant continent; and it is from this, among other causes, that the great mass of the people of this country are distinguished for the very qualities we should look for in emigrants. The same spirit which sent our fathers across the ocean impels us over the Alleghenies, to the valley of the Mississippi, and thence over the Rocky mountains into Oregon.

Indebted to Immigrants

For what are we not indebted to foreign emigration, since we are all Europeans or their descendants? We cannot travel on one of our steamboats without remembering that Robert Fulton was the son of an Irishman. We cannot walk by St. Paul's churchyard without seeing the monuments which admiration and gratitude have erected to Emmet, and [Richard] Montgomery. Who of the thousands who every summer pass up and down our great thoroughfare, the North River, fails to catch at least a passing glimpse of the column erected to the memory of Thaddeus Kosciusko? I cannot forget that only last night a portion of our citizens celebrated with joyous festivities the birthday of the son of Irish emigrants, I mean the Hero of New Orleans [Andrew Jackson]!

Who speaks contemptuously of Alexander Hamilton as a foreigner, because he was born in one of the West India Islands? Who at this day will question the worth or patriotism of Albert Gallatin, because he first opened his eyes among the Alps of Switzerland—though, in fact, this was brought up and urged against him, when he was appointed special minister to Russia by James Madison. What New Yorker applies the epithet of " degraded foreigner" to the German immigrant, John Jacob Astor, a man who has spread his canvas on every sea, drawn to his adopted land the wealth of every clime, and given us, it may be, our best claim to vast territories!

Who would have banished the Frenchman, Stephen Girard, who, after accumulating vast wealth from foreign commerce, endowed with it magnificent institutions for education in his adopted land? So might I go on for hours, citing individual examples of benefits derived by this country from foreign immigration. . . .

The "Harms" of Immigration

I have enumerated some of the advantages which such emigration has given to America. Let us now very carefully inquire, whether there is danger of any injury arising from these causes, at all proportionable to the palpable good.

"Our country is in danger," is the cry of Nativism. During my brief existence I have seen this country on the very verge of ruin a considerable number of times. It is always in the most imminent peril every four years; but, hitherto, the efforts of one party or the other have proved sufficient to rescue it, just in the latest gasp of its expiring agonies, and we have breathed more freely, when we have been assured that "the country's safe." Let us look steadily in the face of this new danger.

Are foreigners coming here to overturn our government? Those who came before the Revolution appear to have been generally favorable to Republican institutions. Those who have come here since have left friends, home, country, all that man naturally holds dearest, that they might live under a free government—they and their children. Is there common sense in the supposition that men would voluntarily set about destroying the very liberties they came so far to enjoy?

"But they lack intelligence," it is said. Are the immigrants of today less intelligent than those of fifty or a hundred years ago? Has Europe and the human race stood still all this time? . . . The facts of men preferring this country to any other, of their desire to live under its institutions, of their migration hither, indicate to my mind anything but a lack of proper intelligence and enterprise. It has been charged against foreigners, by a portion of the whig press, that they generally vote with the democratic party. Allowing this to be so, I think that those who reflect upon the policy of the two parties, from the time of John Adams down to that of Mayor Harper, will scarcely bring this up as the proof of a lack of intelligence!

The truth is, a foreigner who emigrates to this country comes here saying, "Where Liberty dwells, there is my country." He sees our free institutions in the strong light of contrast. The sun seems brighter, because he has come out of darkness. What we know by hearsay only of the superiority of our institutions, he knows by actual observation and experience. Hence it is that America has had no truer patriots—freedom no more enthusiastic admirers—the cause of liberty no more heroic defenders, than have been found among our adopted citizens. . . .

But if naturalized citizens of foreign birth had the disposition, they have not the power, to endanger our liberties, on account of their comparatively small and decreasing numbers. There appears to be a most extraordinary misapprehension upon this subject. To read one of our "Native" papers one might suppose that our country was becoming overrun by foreigners, and that there was real danger of their having a majority of votes. . . .

Immigration Is Insignificant

There is a point beyond which immigration cannot be carried. It must be limited by the capacity of the vessels employed in bringing passengers, while our entire population goes on increasing in geometrical progression, so that in one century from now, we shall have a population of one hundred and sixty millions, but a few hundred thousands of whom at the utmost can be citizens of foreign birth. Thus it may be seen that foreign immigration is of very little account, beyond a certain period, in the population of a country, and at all times is an insignificant item. . . .

In the infancy of this country the firstborn native found himself among a whole colony of foreigners. Now, the foreigner finds himself surrounded by as great a disproportion of natives, and the native babe and newly landed foreigner have about the same amount, of either power or disposition, to endanger the country in which they have arrived; one, because he chose to come—the other because he could not help it.

I said the power or the disposition, for I have yet to learn that foreigners, whether German or Irish, English or French, are at all disposed to do an injury to the asylum which wisdom has prepared and valor won for the oppressed of all nations and religions. I appeal to the observation of every man in this community, whether the Germans and the Irish here, and throughout the country, are not as orderly, as industrious, as quiet, and in the habit of performing as well the common duties of citizens as the great mass of natives among us.

The worst thing that can be brought against any portion of our foreign population is that in many cases they are poor, and when they sink under labor and privation, they have no resources but the almshouse. Alas! shall the rich, for whom they have labored, the owners of the houses they have helped to build, refuse to treat them as kindly as they would their horses when incapable of further toil? Can they grudge them shelter from the storm, and a place where they may die in peace?

> *"The mighty tides of immigration . . . bring to us not only different languages, opinions, customs, and principles, but hostile races, religions, and interests."*

America Should Discourage Immigration (1849)

Garrett Davis

In the 1820s and 1830s the rate of immigration to the United States increased dramatically, with Ireland and Germany replacing Great Britain as the main source of immigrants. Many Americans became concerned about the potential negative effects of this increase in immigration. The following viewpoint is taken from an 1849 speech by Garrett Davis (1801–1872) in which he argues that immigrants endanger America. He contends that the United States should discourage immigration and should restrict immigrants' right to vote. Davis served as a U.S. senator and congressman for the state of Kentucky.

As you read, consider the following questions:
1. How does Davis describe America's newest immigrants?
2. What predictions does Davis make concerning Europe and the United States?
3. What connection does the author make concerning immigration and slavery?

Garrett Davis, speech delivered to the Convention to Revise the Constitution of Kentucky, December 15, 1849.

Why am I opposed to the encouragement of foreign immigration into our country, and disposed to apply any proper checks to it? Why do I propose to suspend to the foreigner, for twenty-one years after he shall have signified formally his intention to become a citizen of the United States, the right of suffrage, the birthright of no man but one native-born? It is because the mighty tides of immigration, each succeeding one increasing in volume, bring to us not only different languages, opinions, customs, and principles, but hostile races, religions, and interests, and the traditionary prejudices of generations with a large amount of the turbulence, disorganizing theories, pauperism, and demoralization of Europe in her redundant population thrown upon us. This multiform and dangerous evil exists and will continue, for "the cry is, Still they come!". . .

The most of those European immigrants, having been born and having lived in the ignorance and degradation of despotisms, without mental or moral culture, with but a vague consciousness of human rights, and no knowledge whatever of the principles of popular constitutional government, their interference in the political administration of our affairs, even when honestly intended, would be about as successful as that of the Indian in the arts and business of civilized private life; and when misdirected, as it would generally be, by bad and designing men, could be productive only of mischief, and from their numbers, of mighty mischief. The system inevitably and in the end will fatally depreciate, degrade, and demoralize the power which governs and rules our destinies.

I freely acknowledge that among such masses of immigrants there are men of noble intellect, of high cultivation, and of great moral worth; men every way adequate to the difficult task of free, popular, and constitutional government. But the number is lamentably small. There can be no contradistinction between them and the incompetent and vicious; and their admission would give no proper compensation, no adequate security against the latter if they, too, were allowed to share political sovereignty. The country could be governed just as wisely and as well by the native-born citizens alone, by which this baleful infusion would be wholly excluded. . . .

The Situation in Europe

This view of the subject is powerfully corroborated by a glance at the state of things in Europe. The aggregate population of that continent in 1807 was 183,000,000. Some years since it was reported to be 260,000,000 and now it is reasonably but little short of 283,000,000; showing an increase within a period of about forty years of 100,000,000. The area of Europe is but little more than that of the United States, and from its higher northern positions and greater proportion of sterile lands, has a less natural capability of sustaining population. All her western, southern, and middle states labor under one of the heaviest afflictions of nations—they have a redundant population. The German states have upward of 70,000,000, and Ireland 8,000,000; all Germany being not larger than three of our largest states, and Ireland being about the size of Kentucky. Daniel O'Connell, in 1843 reported 2,385,000 of the Irish people in a state of destitution. The annual increase of population in Germany and Ireland is in the aggregate near 2,000,000; and in all Europe it is near 7,000,000. Large masses of these people, in many countries, not only want the comforts of life, but its subsistence, its necessaries, and are literally starving. England, many of the German powers, Switzerland, and other governments, have put into operation extensive and well-arranged systems of emigrating and transporting to America their excess of population, and particularly the refuse, the pauper, the demoralized, and the criminal. Very many who come are stout and industrious, and go to labor steadily and thriftily. They send their friends in the old country true and glowing accounts of ours, and with it the means which they have garnered here to bring, too, those friends. Thus, immigration itself increases its means, and constantly adds to its swelling tides. Suppose some mighty convulsion of nature should loosen Europe, the smaller country, from her ocean-deep foundations, and drift her to our coast, would we be ready to take her teeming myriads to our fraternal embrace and give them equally our political sovereignty? If we did, in a few fleeting years where would be the noble Anglo-American race, where their priceless heritage of liberty, where their free constitution, where the best and brightest hopes of man? All would have perished! It is true all Europe is not coming to the United States, but much, too much of it, is; and a dangerous disproportion of the most ignorant and worst of it, without bringing us any territory for them; enough, if they go on increasing and to increase, and are to share with us our power, to bring about such a deplorable result. The question is, Shall they come and take possession of our country and our government, and rule us, or will we, who have the right, rule them and ourselves? I go openly, manfully, and perseveringly for the latter rule, and if it cannot be successfully asserted in all the United States, I am for taking measures to maintain it in Kentucky, and while we can. Now is the time—prevention is easier than cure.

A Surplus Population

The governments of Europe know better than we do that they have a great excess of population. They feel more intensely its great and manifold evils, and for years they have been devising and applying correctives, which have all been mainly resolved into one—to drain off into America their surplus, and especially their destitute, demoralized, and vicious population. By doing so, they not only make more room and comfort for the residue, but they think—and with some truth—that they provide for their own security, and do something to avert explosions which might hurl kings from their thrones. . . .

We have a country of vast extent, with a great variety of climate, soil, production, industry, and pursuit. Competing interests and sectional questions are a natural and fruitful source

---

Imminent Peril

It is an incontrovertible truth that the civil institutions of the United States of America have been seriously affected, and that they now stand in imminent peril from the rapid and enormous increase of the body of residents of foreign birth, imbued with foreign feelings, and of an ignorant and immoral character, who receive, under the present lax and unreasonable laws of naturalization, the elective franchise and the right of eligibility to political office.

Declaration of the Native American National Convention, July 4, 1845.

---

of jealousies, discords, and factions. We have about four millions of slaves, and the slaveholding and free states are nearly equally divided in number, but the population of the latter greatly preponderating, and every portion of it deeply imbued with inflexible hostility to slavery as an institution. Even now conflict of opinion and passion of the two great sections of the Union upon the subject of slavery is threatening to rend this Union, and change confederated states and one people into hostile and warring powers. Cession [by Mexico of the Upper California, Utah, and New Mexico territories] has recently given to us considerable numbers of the Spanish race, and a greatly increasing immigration is constantly pouring in upon us the hordes of Europe, with their hereditary national animosities, their discordant races, languages, and religious faiths, their ignorance and their pauperism, mixed up with a large amount of idleness, moral degradation, and crime; and all this "heterogeneous, discordant, distracted mass," to use Mr. Jefferson's language, "sharing with us the legislation" and the entire political sovereignty. . . .

Washington and Jefferson and their associates, though among the wisest and most far-seeing of mankind, could not but descry in the future many formidable difficulties and dangers, and thus be premonished to provide against them in fashioning our institutions. If they had foreseen the vast, the appalling increase of immigration upon us at the present, there can be no reasonable doubt that laws to naturalize the foreigners and to give up to them the country, its liberties, its destiny, would not have been authorized by the constitution. The danger, though great, is not wholly without remedy. We can do something if we do it quickly. The German and Slavonic races are combining in the state of New York to elect candidates of their own blood to Congress. This is the beginning of the conflict of races on a large scale, and it must, in the nature of things, continue and increase. It must be universal and severe in all the field of labor, between the native and the stranger, and from the myriads of foreign laborers coming to us, if it does not become a contest for bread and subsistence, wages will at least be brought down so low as to hold our native laborers and their families in hopeless poverty. They cannot adopt the habits of life and

The Dangers of Foreigners

The rapid increase of any nation, by means of an influx of foreigners, is dangerous to the repose of that nation; especially if the number of emigrants bears any considerable proportion to the old inhabitants. Even if that proportion is very small, the tendency of the thing is injurious, unless the newcomers are more civilized and more virtuous, and have at the same time, the same ideas and feeling about government. But if they are more vicious, they will corrupt; if less industrious, they will promote idleness; if they have different ideas of government, they will contend, if the same, they will intrigue and interfere.

Samuel Whelpley, *A Compend of History from the Earliest Time, Comprehending a General View of the Present State of the World*, 1825.

---

live upon the stinted meager supplies to which the foreigner will restrict himself, and which is bounteous plenty to what he has been accustomed in the old country. Already these results are taking place in many of the mechanic arts. Duty, patriotism, and wisdom all require us to protect the labor, and to keep up to a fair scale the wages of our native-born people as far as by laws and measures of public policy it can be done. The foreigner, too, is the natural foe of the slavery of our state. He is opposed to it by all his past associations, and when he comes to our state he sees 200,000 laborers of a totally different race to himself excluding him measurably from employment and wages. He hears a measure agitated to send these 200,000 competitors away. Their exodus will make room for him, his kindred and race, and create such a demand for labor, as he will reason it, to give him high wages. He goes naturally for the measure, and becomes an emancipationist. While the slave is with us, the foreigner will not crowd us, which will postpone to a long day the affliction of nations, an excess of population; the slaves away, the great tide of immigration will set in upon us, and precipitate upon our happy land this, the chief misery of most of the countries of Europe. Look at the myriads who are perpetually pouring into the northwestern states from the German hives—making large and exclusive settlements for themselves, which in a few years will number their thousands and tens of thousands, living in isolation; speaking a strange language, having alien manners, habits, opinions, and religious faiths, and a total ignorance of our political institutions; all handed down with German phlegm and inflexibility to their children through generations. In less than fifty years, northern Illinois, parts of Ohio, and Michigan, Wisconsin, Iowa, and Minnesota will be literally possessed by them; they will number millions and millions, and they will be essentially a distinct people, a nation within a nation, a new Germany. We can't keep these people wholly out, and ought not if we could; but we are getting more than our share of them. I wish they would turn their direction to South America, quite as good a portion of the world as our share of the hemisphere. They could there aid in bringing up the slothful and degenerate Spanish race; here their deplorable office is to pull us down. Our proud boast is that the Anglo-Saxon race is the first among all the world of man, and that we are a shoot from this noble stock; but how long will we be as things are progressing? In a few years, as a distinctive race, the Anglo-Americans will be as much lost to the world and its future history as the lost tribes of Israel. . . .

No well-informed and observant man can look abroad over this widespread and blessed country without feeling deep anxiety for the future. Some elements of discord and disunion are even now in fearful action. Spread out to such a vast extent, filling up almost in geometrical progression with communities and colonies from many lands, various as Europe in personal and national characteristics, in opinions, in manners and customs, in tongues and religious faiths, in the traditions of the past, and the objects and the hopes of the future, the United States can, no more than Europe, become one homogeneous mass—one peaceful, united, harmonizing, all self-adhering people. When the country shall begin to teem with people, these jarring elements being brought into proximity, their repellent and explosive properties will begin to act with greater intensity; and then, if not before, will come the war of geographical sections, the war of races, and the most relentless of all wars, of hostile religions. This mournful catastrophe will have been greatly hastened by our immense expansion and our proclamation to all mankind to become a part of us.

"By restricting immigration we . . . will give to a large body of citizens a decent and comfortable standard of living."

Restrictions on Immigration Are Necessary (1913)

Frank Julian Warne

The late 1800s and early 1900s were peak years for immigration to the United States. Many of these immigrants came from southern and eastern Europe, and their arrival rekindled debates over immigration. Some Americans argued that these new arrivals were racially inferior, while others said immigrants took away jobs and depressed wages. The following viewpoint is excerpted from the book *The Immigrant Invasion* by Frank Julian Warne (1874–1948). Focusing on economics instead of race, Warne states that the influx of immigrants is creating a lower standard of living for all Americans. He maintains that the United States needs national legislation restricting immigration. An economist and author, Warne served as a special expert on immigrants for the 1910 U.S. Census.

As you read, consider the following questions:
1. What is the central issue of immigration, according to Warne?
2. How does the author respond to the argument that immigrants take jobs other people do not want?
3. What kinds of new laws on immigration does Warne propose?

Frank Julian Warne, *The Immigrant Invasion*. New York: Dodd, Mead, and Company, 1913.

D ifferent people studying and observing the immigration phenomenon do not always see the same thing—they receive different impressions from it. Sometimes the other view is apparent to their consciousness but usually their mind is so taken up with their own view that the other is of lesser significance.

Two Views of Immigration

One view of immigration is that which is conspicuous to the worker who has been and is being driven out of his position by the immigrant; to members of the labour union struggling to control this competition and to maintain their standard of living; to those who see the socially injurious and individually disastrous effects upon the American worker of this foreign stream of cheap labour; to those who know the pauperising effects of a low wage, long hours of work, and harsh conditions of employment; to those personally familiar with the poverty in many of our foreign "colonies"; to those acquainted with the congested slum districts in our large industrial centres and cities and the innumerable problems which they present; to those who long and strive for an early realisation of Industrial Democracy. . . .

The other view is seen, however, by those who believe that the immigrant is escaping from intolerable religious, racial, and political persecution and oppression; whose sympathies have been aroused by a knowledge of the adverse economic conditions of the masses of Europe; by those immigrants and their children already here who desire to have their loved ones join them; by producers and manufacturers seeking cheap labour; by those holding bonds and stocks in steamship companies receiving large revenues from the transportation of the immigrant; by those who see subjects of European despotism transformed into naturalised citizens of the American republic, with all that this implies for them and for their children.

The so-called good side of immigration is seen primarily from the viewpoint of the immigrant himself. Any perspective of immigration through the eyes of the alien must necessarily, as a rule, be an optimistic one. Although some of them are possibly worse off in the United States than if they had remained in their European home, at the same time the larger number improve their condition by coming to America. Let us admit, then, that immigration benefits the immigrant.

Thus are indicated two views of immigration. These opposite views are very rapidly dividing the American people into two camps or parties—those who favour a continuance of our present liberal policy and those who are striving to have laws passed that will further restrict immigration. The different groups are made up for the most part of well-intentioned people looking at identically the same national problem but who see entirely different aspects or effects. . . .

The Real Issue

Those who are desirous of settling the immigration question solely from the point of view of the best interests of the country are quite frequently sidetracked from the only real and fundamental argument into the discussion of relatively unimportant phases of it. The real objection to immigration at the present time lies not in the fact that Slavs and Italians and Greeks and Syrians instead of Irish and Germans and English are coming to the United States. Nor does it lie in the fact that the immigrants are or become paupers and criminals. The real objection has nothing to do with the composition of our immigration stream, nor with the characteristics of the individuals or races composing it. It is more than likely that the evils so prominent today would still exist if we had received the Slavs and Italians fifty years ago and were receiving the English and Irish and Germans at the present day.

The real objection to immigration lies in the changed conditions that have come about in the United States themselves. These conditions now dominate and control the tendencies that immigration manifests. At the present time they are giving to the country a surplus of cheap labour—a greater supply than our industries and manufacturing enterprises need. In consequence this over-supply has brought into play among our industrial toilers the great law of competition. This economic law is controlled by the more recent immigrant because of his immediate necessity to secure employment and his ability to sell his labour at a low price—to work for a low wage. Against the operation of this law the native worker and the earlier immigrant are unable to defend themselves. It is affecting detrimentally the standard of living of hundreds of thousands of workers—workers, too, who are also citizens, fathers, husbands.

Immigrants and Machines

But who will do the rough work that must be done if we cannot get the immigrant? asks the liberal immigrationist. And to clinch his argument he goes into raptures over the industrial characteristics of the immigrant and points out enthusiastically the important part the alien has played in America's material upbuilding.

Immigration tends to retard the invention and introduction of machinery which otherwise would do this rough work for us. It has prevented capital in our industries from giving the proper amount of attention to the increase and use of machines, says Professor John R. Commons in "Races and Immigrants in America."

> The cigar-making machine cannot extensively be introduced on the Pacific coast because Chinese cheap labour makes the same cigars at less cost than the machines. High wages stimulate the invention and use of machinery and scientific processes, and it is machinery and science, more than mere hand labour, on which reliance must be placed to develop the natural resources of a country. But machinery and science cannot be as quickly introduced as cheap immigrant labour. . . . In the haste to get profits the immigrant is more desired than machinery.

As long as cheap labour is available this tendency will continue. Even in spite of the large supply of immigrants who work for a low wage, what has already been accomplished along the line of adapting machinery to do the rough work is but indicative of what would be done in this direction if immigration were restricted. . . .

U.S. Immigration Hurts Other Countries

When anyone suggests the restriction of immigration to those who believe in throwing open wide our gates to all the races of the world, the conclusion is immediately arrived at that the proposer has some personal feeling in the matter and that he is not in sympathy with the immigrant. As a matter of fact the restriction of immigration is herein suggested not alone from the point of view of the future political development of the United States, but also from that of the interest and welfare of the immigrant himself and his descendants. It is made in order to prevent them from becoming in the future an industrial slave class in America and to assist them in throwing off in their European homes the shackles which now bind them and are the primary cause of their securing there so little from an abundant world.

Unite to Reduce Immigration

It is the duty of all Americans from Maine to Texas and from Washington to Florida to forget the dissensions of the past and unite in an effort to reduce immigration to the lowest possible point or stop it altogether, and to compel the foreigners now here either to accept our traditions and ideals or else to return to the land from which they came, by deportation or otherwise.

Madison Grant, *The Alien in Our Midst*, 1930.

One of the strongest arguments in the past of the liberal immigrationist is that the downtrodden and oppressed of Europe are fleeing from intolerable economic, political, and religious conditions into a land of liberty and freedom which offers opportunities to all. It may be very much questioned if these immigrants are finding here the hoped-for escape from oppression and servitude and exploitation, for since the newer immigration began in the eighties there has come to dwell in America a horrible modern Frankenstein in the shape of the depressing conditions surrounding a vast majority of our industrial toilers. But even granting that the immigrants coming to us do better their condition, a very pertinent question is as to the effect the prevention of this immigration would have upon the countries from which it comes. If we grant that the immigrants are able-bodied, disposed to resent oppression and are striving to better their condition, are they not the very ones that should remain in their European homes and there through growing restlessness and increasing power change for the better the conditions from which they are fleeing? As it is now, instead of an improvement in those conditions the stronger and more able-bodied—the ones better able to cope with them and improve them—are running away and leaving behind the less able and weaker members, who continue to live under the intolerable conditions.

If immigration to the United States were stopped one would not likely be far wrong in prophesying that either one of two things would happen in these European countries: Either a voluntary remedying by the European Governments themselves of political, religious, and economic evils, or else those countries would soon be confronted by revolutions springing from this unrest of the people which now finds an escape through emigration to the United States. . . . Pent up discontent, unrelieved by emigration, would burst its bounds to the betterment of the general social conditions of the European masses.

Another phase of this same aspect of immigration is the fact that indirectly the United States which, if it stands for anything, stands in opposition to nearly all that is represented by the European form of government—this country, to a considerable extent, helps to keep in power these very governments against which it is a living protest. This is done in one way through the enormous sums of money that immigrants in the United States send each year to the European countries.

It is estimated that from two hundred to two hundred and fifty million dollars are sent abroad annually to the more important European countries by the foreign born in the United States. Part of this enormous sum finds its way by direct and indirect taxation into the coffers of the Government and the Bureaucracy and thus tends to support and continue them in power. When this fact is kept in mind—the fact that nearly two hundred and fifty million dollars are sent abroad each year by immigrants in the United States—it is an argument that answers thoroughly the claim of large employers of labour that immigration is an advantage to the country in that it brings to us annually through the immigrant nearly $25,000,000. The fact is that an amount nine times greater than that brought in is sent out of the country each year by the immigrant. . . .

Needed: More Restrictions

Virtually all objection or opposition to any suggestion as to immigration restriction comes from the immigrant races themselves. As for the attitude of the native, he seems for the greater part to be apathetic when it comes to taking some practical action to remedy conditions, although his grumbling and open opposition is becoming louder than ever before.

Our present statutes, except as they relate to labourers brought in under contract, exclude only such manifestly undesirable persons as idiots, the insane, paupers, immigrants likely to become a public charge, those with loathsome or dangerous contagious diseases, persons whose physical or mental defects prevent them from earning a living, convicted criminals, prostitutes, and the like. Even a strict enforcement of these laws makes it possible to keep out only the poorest and worst elements in these groups who come here.

Referring to the fact that certain undesirable immigrants are not being reached by the present laws the Commissioner of Immigration at Ellis Island, Mr. William Williams, says:

We have no statutes excluding those whose economic condition is so low that their competition tends to reduce the standard of our wage worker, nor those who flock to the congested districts of our large cities where their presence may not be needed, in place of going to the country districts where immigrants of the right type are needed. As far back as 1901 reference was made by President Roosevelt in his annual message to Congress to those foreign labourers who 'represent a standard of living so depressed that they can undersell our men in the labour market and drag them to a lower level,' and it was recommended that 'all persons should be excluded who are below a certain standard of economic fitness to enter our industrial fields as competitors with American labourers.' There are no laws under which aliens of the class described can be kept out unless they happen to fall within one of the classes now excluded by statutes (as they sometimes do); and yet organised forces are at work, principally on the other side of the ocean, to induce many to come here whose standards of living are so low that it is detrimental to the best interests of the country that the American labourers should be compelled to compete with them.

To regulate, and this means to restrict immigration so that we may continue to receive its benefits while at the same time the welfare of the country is safeguarded against its evils, is the issue. . . .

Immigration Should Cease

I have become convinced that the safety of our institutions, the continuity of our prosperity, the preservation of our standards of living, and the maintaining of a decent level of morals among us depends upon a most rigid limitation of immigration and the maintaining of a rigid standard as to even those few who may be admitted.

Albert Johnson, *The Alien in Our Midst*, 1930.

It is a curious fact, but none the less a fact, that too much, even of something that in moderate amounts is good for us, may become very injurious—so injurious as to necessitate the regulation of the quantity we should have. The quantity of present immigration is no bugaboo but a real danger threatening most seriously the success of "The American Experiment" in government and social organisation. It is such as to over-tax our wonderful powers of assimilation. . . .

In the case of the immigration stream now pouring in huge volume into the United States, have we, through our public schools and like safeguards, erected a sufficiently strong dam to protect our institutions? Our forefathers bequeathed to us an educational system that was designed and which was supposed to be strong enough to withstand any flood of ignorance that might beat against our institutions. But this system was not devised in any of its particulars to care for the great volume of ignorance which is now washing into the United States with tremendous force from out of eastern and southern Europe. In many respects it is even now too late to strengthen this educational system. What effect is this volume of ignorance, which is breaking in and overflowing our safeguards, to have on political and religious structures and our social and national life? . . .

The American Republic, with its valuable institutions, approaches the parting of the ways. Fortunately the writing on the signboards is plain. The choice the people are to make as to which way they shall go will determine the kind of civilisation that is to have its home in the United States for coming generations. This choice has to be made—there is no way out of it. It will be made even if no political or governmental action is taken. In this case the choice will be to continue our present policy of unrestricted immigration in cheap labour. This will mean a continuance of the development in feverish haste of the country's material resources by an inpouring of labourers with low standards of living and the perpetuation of a debased citizenship among both the exploited and the exploiters.

The alternative is to restrict immigration so that we can catch our breath and take an inventory of what we already have among us that must imperatively be raised to a higher standard of living and a safer citizenship.

America's Choice

Our decision means a choice between two conditions. By continuing our present policy we choose that which is producing a plutocratic caste class of idle nobodies resting upon the industrial slavery of a great mass of ignorant and low standard of living toilers. By restricting immigration we influence the bringing about of a condition that will give to a large body of citizens a decent and comfortable standard of living. This desired result is to be obtained by a more just distribution of wealth through wages and prices and dividends.

"Immigration to the United States suffers from too much legislation."

Restrictions on Immigration Are Not Necessary (1912)

Peter Roberts

Peter Roberts (1859–1932) was a Congregationalist pastor and the author of several books on immigrants. The following viewpoint is excerpted from *The New Immigration*, a study of immigrants from southern and eastern Europe first published in 1912. Roberts argues that these immigrants have been beneficial to the United States. He maintains that more legislation restricting immigration is unnecessary and calls for Americans to accept these new immigrants.

As you read, consider the following questions:
1. In the author's opinion, how are commonly accepted stereotypes of immigrants incorrect?
2. According to the author, how do immigrants affect jobs and wages?
3. What does the United States suffer from, according to Roberts?

Peter Roberts, *The New Immigration*. New York: Arno Press, 1970.

All students of immigration should try to do two things: first, get the facts, argue from them, and discard popular prejudices and antipathies—we want to know conditions as they are and not as the biased imagine them to be; second, not to lay at the door of the foreigners evils and conditions which are due to the cupidity, short-sightedness, and inefficiency of the native-born.

"The Scum of the Earth"

The statements that the millions of "the distressed and unfortunate of other lands and climes," "the scum of Europe," "the beaten men of beaten races," "the inefficient, impoverished, and diseased," seek American shores, are untrue, uncharitable, and malicious. Emigration from any land, taken as a whole, is made up of the most vigorous, enterprising, and strongest members of the race. No one denies this when the character of the immigrants who came to America in 1820–1880 is discussed. Censors and prophets of evil proclaimed the stereotyped catalogue of calamities when they came, but their fears were not realized; the men made good and their children are an honor to the nation. The men of the new immigration are now under the eye of the censor, and the prophets of calamities are not wanting, but those who know the newer immigrants intimately believe that they, as their predecessors, will make good and that their children will be an honor to us, if the same opportunities are given these men and thirty years of American influences are allowed to shape and mold their lives. In the winning of the West, the Atlantic states lost much of its best blood by migration, and the same may be said of the exodus of young men from southeastern European countries to America. Every European government, losing its workers by emigration, bemoans the fact and is looking around for some means to check the outflow of strong manhood: would any of them do this if the "scum," "the unfortunate," "the beaten" emigrated?. . .

The slums of Europe are not sent here. The facts and figures of immigration to the United States clearly show that the men of the new immigration come from the farm, and they compare favorably in bodily form and strength with men raised in agricultural communities elsewhere. In the stream, undesirables are found, but the percentage is low. Taken as a whole, they do not show moral turpitude above the average of civilized men. Although transplanted into a new environment, living under abnormal conditions in industrial centers, and meeting more temptations in a week than they would in a lifetime in rural communities in the homeland, yet when their criminal record is compared with that of the native born males, it comes out better than even.

All the immigrants landed do not stay here. In the decade 1900–1910, 8,795,386 arrived, but the last census enumerators only found 13,343,583 foreign-born in the United States, as against 10,213,817, in 1900. These figures clearly indicate that little more than 60 per cent of the total arrivals of that decade were in the country in 1910. A large percentage of this returning stream represents men and women who could not stand the stress and strain of American life; or, in other words, the unfit were more carefully weeded out by industrial competition than by the laws regulating immigration. This again works in favor of virile accretions to the population of the United States.

Composition of Immigrants by Decades

	From Northwest Europe	From Southeast Europe	All Others
	Per Cent	Per Cent	Per Cent
1821–1830	76.5	8.0	15.5
1831–1840	84.3	10.0	5.7
1841–1850	93.4	5.1	1.5
1851–1860	93.3	4.3	2.4
1861–1870	85.5	10.9	3.6
1871–1880	72.0	16.5	11.5
1881–1890	68.0	18.9	12.1
1891–1900	48.2	51.0	2.8
1901–1910	26.1	65.9	8.0

Peter Roberts, *The New Immigration*, 1912.

We constantly hear about the stream of gold going to Europe, which reached high-water mark in 1907, the year when immigration exceeded a million and a quarter, and the industrial boom was at its height. In that year, the Immigration Commission estimated the amount of money sent back to Europe at $275,000,000. America is a great country, and this sum should be compared with our industrial and commercial importance. The value of the coal mined that year was nearly two and a half times larger than the sum sent to Europe; the products of our mines were eight times as valuable; our commerce with foreign countries aggregated a sum more than eleven times as great; the value of the produce of the farms of the United States was twenty-one times as great; the value of the products of our manufacturing was fifty times larger; and if we compare the sum sent by immigrants to Europe during this year of prosperity with the total estimated wealth of the nation in 1907, it is about two-tenths of one per cent. Can the economists and statesmen, who, in this great country of ours, become excited over this item, as if the welfare of America depended upon its retention on this side of the water, be taken seriously? We don't think they take themselves seriously. . . .

But we are told that "the immigrants most dangerous are those who come . . . to earn the *higher wages* offered in the United States, with the fixed intention of returning to their families in the home country to spend those wages." The fact is, that the immigrants earn the *lower wages* offered in the United States, suffer most from intermittent and seasonal labor, and, being largely employed in hazardous industries, pay the major part of the loss of life and limb incident to these operations. The country owes a debt to every immigrant who returns having spent many years of his life in our industrial army. . . .

The Standard of Living

We are also told that the foreigners have reduced wages and affected the American standard of living. On the first point, the Department of Commerce and Labor, after long and patient investigation, has failed to find a reduction in wage in the industries largely manned by immigrants.

Is it not a fact that wages were never as high in the industries of the United States as in 1907, the year when immigration touched high-water mark and 1,285,349 came to

The Declaration of Independence

A little attention to the principles involved would have convinced us long ago that an American citizen who preaches wholesale restriction of immigration is guilty of political heresy. The Declaration of Independence accords to *all* men an equal share in the inherent rights of humanity. When we go contrary to that principle, we are not acting as Americans; for, by definition, an American is one who lives by the principles of the Declaration. And we surely violate the Declaration when we attempt to exclude aliens on account of race, nationality, or economic status. "*All* men" means yellow men as well as white men, men from the South of Europe as well as men from the North of Europe, men who hold kingdoms in pawn, and men who owe for their dinner. We shall have to recall officially the Declaration of Independence before we can lawfully limit the application of its principles to this or that group of men.

Mary Antin, *They Who Knock at Our Gates*, 1914.

America? The immigrants from southeastern Europe, when they understand what the standard wage is, will fight for it with far greater solidarity than the Anglo-Saxon or the Teuton. The most stubborn strikes in recent years have been the anthracite coal strike, the McKees Rocks, the Westmoreland, etc., in each of which the men of the new immigration were in the majority. It would be difficult to give concrete instances of foreigners actually reducing wages, but many instances may be given where they have stubbornly resisted a reduction and bravely fought for an increased wage. As to the second point, the American standard of living is a shifting one. In the mill towns and mine patches of West Virginia, North Carolina, and Alabama, the foreigners would have to come down many degrees in order to conform with the standard of living of Americans of purest blood. In a town in New England, a banker said that the New England Yankee was in his capacity to save money a close second to the Magyar, who led the foreigners in this respect. Put the native-born on $450 a year—the average wage of foreigners—and will he be able to build a home, raise a family, and push the children several degrees up in the economic scale? The immigrants are doing this. Suppose the new immigration had kept away, would the wages of unskilled labor be higher? This leads us to the region of conjecture. One thing we know, that the wage has steadily advanced notwithstanding the unprecedented inflow of the last decade. . . .

We are further told that "the immigrants are not *additional* inhabitants," but that "their coming displaces the native stock"; "that the racial suicide is closely connected with the problem of immigration." If "racial suicide" were a phenomenon peculiar to the United States, there would be force in the argument. There is no immigration into France, and yet sterility and a low birth rate have been the concern of statesmen and moralists in that country for the last quarter of a century. The same phenomenon is observed among the middle classes in England and the Scandinavian peninsula. Artificial restriction on natality is practiced in every industrial country by men and women whose income is such that they must choose between raising a family or maintaining their social status. One or the other of these two institutions must suffer and it is generally the family. This is the case in America. The native-born clerk, tradesman, machinist, professional man, etc., whose income ranges between $800 and $1200 a year, can hardly risk matrimony in an urban community. If he does take a wife, they can hardly afford to raise one child, while two cause great anxiety. A low birth rate is a condition that is superinduced by industrial development. The opportunity for advancement, social prestige, love of power and its retention in the family, etc., these are some of the causes of a low birth rate. "But greater than any other cause is 'the deliberate and voluntary avoidance of child-bearing on the part of a steadily increasing number of married people, who not only prefer to have but few children, but who know how to obtain their wish,'" [according to W.B. Bailey]. Immigration is no more the cause of racial suicide than the countryside superstition that a plentiful crop of nuts is the cause of fecundity. . . .

Immigrants Do Needed Work

The foreigners are despised for the work they do. Must this work be done? Can America get along without sewer digging, construction work, tunnel driving, coal mining, meat packing, hide tanning, etc.—disagreeable work, which the

English-speaking shun? This labor is necessary and the foreigners do it uncomplainingly. Should they be condemned, despised, and dubbed "the scum of the earth" for doing basic work which we all know is a necessity, but which we ourselves will not perform? A percentage of foreigners is illiterate, and a still larger percentage is unskilled, but every one who has studied these men knows that they have common sense, meekness, patience, submission, docility, and gratitude—qualities which have made them admirably suited for the coarse work America needs done. The accident of birth accounts largely for skill in reading and writing as well as for a knowledge of the trades: we cannot choose the country of our birth any more than hereditary tendencies; why, then, should we blame men for the consequence of these accidents? The best judges of America's need of unskilled labor are employers, men of affairs, and leaders in the industrial development of the nation, and these without exception say that the foreigner has been a blessing and not a curse. In 1910, the National Board of Trade received letters from ninety-three such men, residing in thirty-five states, expressing their views as to the effect of immigration on labor and the industries, and the following is the summary of their answers:—

1. That the general effect of immigration to this country has been beneficial.

2. That immigration so far has not constituted a menace to American labor.

3. That it is still needed for our industrial and commercial development.

In view of these conclusions, the right of the foreigner to respect and honorable treatment from Americans ought to be acknowledged; the credit due him for the part he has played in the industrial development of America should be freely given; his right to the free enjoyment of the fruit of his labor wherever he chooses to spend his money should be conceded; but unfortunately none of these rights is recognized by a vast number of native-born men in the immigration zone. . . .

We have reason to believe that immigration to the United States suffers from too much legislation. Multiplicity of laws

Immigrants and Prosperity

The economic supremacy of the United States was attained during the very period when large numbers of immigrants were coming into the country. . . .

Immigrants have contributed greatly to the industrial development of this country; contributed not alone by their numbers but also by their age, sex and training.

Constantine Panunzio, *Immigration Crossroads*, 1927.

will not secure to the United States immunity from the evils of immigration. Each new barrier erected invites the cunning and duplicity of shrewd foreigners to overcome it and affords an opportunity to exploit the ignorant. It is the duty of the government to guard the gates against the diseased, the insane, and the criminal, and our present laws, in the hands of competent men, do this. The immigrant has a right to look for transportation conveniences on steamships and accommodations in detention stations, which comply with the demands of sanitary science and personal hygiene. Every important distributing center should have detention halls, where the immigrants could be kept until called for by friends or guided by responsible parties to their destination. America collects $4 per head from all immigrants coming to the country. Canada spends that amount per head to give the newcomers the necessary information as to agricultural opportunities and economic conditions, so that the men may exercise their judgement as to place to locate and employment to seek. The immigrants will never be distributed in the states and the communities where their labor would count for most, as long as the hands of the division of information of the Bureau of Immigration are tied by the want of funds to fulfill the purpose for which it was created. The attempt to regulate the inflow of immigrants by legislation according to the labor supply of this country is impracticable and will inevitably lead to political skirmishing. Who is to decide the condition of the labor market, the operators or the trades-union? Economic law will regulate this far more effectually and promptly. While the recommendations of the Immigration Commission wait the action of Congress, industrial depression has driven 2,000,000 workers out of the country. If the "Conclusions and Recommendations" of the Commission were written in 1907 instead of 1910, their tone would be very different. A few efficient laws left alone and well executed are better than many statutes, continuous legislative tinkering, and inefficiency.

The assimilation of the immigrants must depend more upon private effort than upon legislation. No action of either Federal or state government can do half as much for aliens wishing to join the family as the conduct of Americans in the immigration zone, who can help this cause more by throwing open the school building than by urging the enactment of state laws concerning the illiteracy of foreigners. Centers opened in every public school in foreign colonies, where immigrants could be taught, would do more for foreigners in one year, than ten years of legislative inhibition as to what the foreigners should or should not do. . . .

Legislative action and private organizations can do much for immigrants, but the most effective of all remedies is personal contact. We can legislate as we have a mind to, but unless the native-born is ready to take the foreign-born in confidence and sympathy into the family, there will be no assimilation. Of the 13,500,000 foreign-born in the country at present, about half of them are from southeastern Europe: in other words in a population of 90,000,000 whites, just one out of every fifteen is a child of the backward races of Europe, and we all stand in awe of him and say he is a menace. Would it not be better to trust the brother, believe that he is capable of infinite good, give him a fair chance in the race, secure to him all freedom of opportunity, and treat him at all times as a responsible moral being with rights and duties as other men? If this personal touch is secured, righteous treatment given, and broad sympathetic interest shown, the immigration problem will be solved in the light of the brotherhood of man and the spirit of our democracy.

*"The use of a national origins system is
without basis in either logic or reason."*

National Origins Quotas
Should Be Abolished (1963)

John F. Kennedy

In 1921 and 1924, Congress passed laws that placed limits on
immigration. These laws awarded each foreign country immigration quotas based on the ethnic composition of the
United States. The effect of the laws, revised but not significantly changed in 1952, was to sharply limit immigration
from southern and eastern Europe, as well as Africa and Asia.
Many people criticized this quota system as being racist and
at odds with American values. In the following viewpoint,
John F. Kennedy (1917–1963) argues that this system of national origins quotas is embarrassing to the United States and
should be eliminated. Kennedy, a great-grandson of Irish immigrants, was elected president of the United States in 1960.
Many of the ideas Kennedy states in this viewpoint were enacted into law in 1965, two years after he was assassinated.

As you read, consider the following questions:
1. What were the motivations behind the immigration laws
   of 1921 and 1924, according to Kennedy?
2. Why are national origins quotas racist, according to the
   author?
3. What reforms to U.S. immigration law does Kennedy
   propose?

John F. Kennedy, *A Nation of Immigrants*. New York: HarperCollins, 1964.

From the start, immigration policy has been a prominent subject of discussion in America. This is as it must be in a democracy, where every issue should be freely considered and debated.

Ambiguous Attitudes

Immigration, or rather the British policy of clamping down on immigration, was one of the factors behind the colonial desire for independence. Restrictive immigration policies constituted one of the charges against King George III expressed in the Declaration of Independence. And in the Constitutional Convention James Madison noted, "That part of America which has encouraged them [the immigrants] has advanced most rapidly in population, agriculture and the arts." So, too, Washington in his Thanksgiving Day Proclamation of 1795 asked all Americans "humbly and fervently to beseech the kind Author of these blessings . . . to render this country more and more a safe and propitious asylum for the unfortunate of other countries."

Yet there was the basic ambiguity which older Americans have often shown toward newcomers. In 1797 a member of Congress argued that, while a liberal immigration policy was fine when the country was new and unsettled, now that America had reached its maturity and was fully populated, immigration should stop—an argument which has been repeated at regular intervals throughout American history. . . .

By the turn of the century the opinion was becoming widespread that the numbers of new immigrants should be limited. Those who were opposed to all immigration and all "foreigners" were now joined by those who believed sincerely, and with some basis in fact, that America's capacity to absorb immigration was limited. This movement toward restricting immigration represented a social and economic reaction, not only to the tremendous increase in immigration after 1880, but also to the shift in its main sources, to Southern, Eastern and Southeastern Europe.

The Quota System

Anti-immigration sentiment was heightened by World War I, and the disillusionment and strong wave of isolationism that marked its aftermath. It was in this climate, in 1921, that Congress passed and the President signed the first major law in our country's history severely limiting new immigration by establishing an emergency quota system. An era in American history had ended, we were committed to a radically new policy toward the peopling of the nation.

The Act of 1921 was an early version of the so-called "national origins" system. Its provisions limited immigration of numbers of each nationality to a certain percentage of the number of foreign-born individuals of that nationality resident in the United States according to the 1910 census. Nationality meant country of birth. The total number of immigrants permitted to enter under this system each year was 357,000.

In 1924 the Act was revised, creating a temporary arrangement for the years 1924 to 1929, under which the national quotas for 1924 were equal to 2 percent of the number of foreign-born persons of a given nationality living in the United States in 1890, or about 164,000 people. The permanent system, which went into force in 1929, includes essentially all the elements of immigration policy that are in our law today. The immigration statutes now establish a system of annual quotas to govern immigration from each country. Under this system 156,987 quota immigrants are permitted to enter the United States each year. The quotas from each country are based upon the national origins of the population of the United States in 1920.

The use of the year 1920 is arbitrary. It rests upon the fact that this system was introduced in 1924 and the last prior census was in 1920. The use of a national origins system is without basis in either logic or reason. It neither satisfies a national need nor accomplishes an international purpose. In an age of interdependence among nations such a system is an anachronism, for it discriminates among applicants for admission into the United States on the basis of accident of birth.

The System Favors Northern Europe

Because of the composition of our population in 1920, the system is heavily weighted in favor of immigration from Northern Europe and severely limits immigration from Southern and Eastern Europe and from other parts of the world.

"What Happened To The One We Used To Have?"

U.S. IMMIGRATION POLICY

HERBLOCK

Herblock. © 1946 by *The Washington Post*. Reprinted with permission.

To cite some examples: Great Britain has an annual quota of 65,361 immigration visas and used 28,291 of them. Germany has a quota of 25,814 and used 26,533 (of this number, about one third are wives of servicemen who could enter on a non-quota basis). Ireland's quota is 17,756 and only 6,054 Irish availed themselves of it. On the other hand, Poland is permitted 6,488, and there is a backlog of 61,293 Poles wishing to enter the United States, Italy is permitted 5,666 and has a backlog of 132,435, Greece's quota is 308; her backlog is 96,538. Thus a Greek citizen desiring to emigrate to this country has little chance of coming here. And an American citizen with a Greek father or mother must wait at least eighteen months to bring his parents here to join him. A citizen whose married son or daughter, or brother or sister, is Italian cannot obtain a quota number for them for two years or more. Meanwhile, many thousands of quota numbers are wasted because they are not wanted or needed by nationals of the countries to which they are assigned.

In short, a qualified person born in England or Ireland who wants to emigrate to the United States can do so at any time. A person born in Italy, Hungary, Poland or the Baltic States may have to wait many years before his turn is reached. This system is based upon the assumption that there is some reason for keeping the origins of our population in exactly the same proportions as they existed in 1920. Such an idea is at complete variance with the American traditions and principles that the qualification of an immigrant do not depend upon his country of birth, and violates the spirit expressed in the Declaration of Independence that "all men are created equal."

One writer has listed six motives behind the Act of 1924. They were: (1) postwar isolationism; (2) the doctrine of the alleged superiority of Anglo Saxon and Teutonic "races"; (3) the fear that "pauper labor" would lower wage levels; (4) the belief that people of certain nations were less law-abiding than others; (5) the fear of foreign ideologies and subversion; (6) the fear that entrance of too many people with different customs and habits would undermine our national and social unity and order. All of these arguments can be found in Congressional debates on the subject and may be heard today in discussions over a new national policy toward immigration. Thus far, they have prevailed. The policy of 1924 was continued in all its essentials by the Immigration and Nationality Act of 1952. . . .

1952 Revisions

The Immigration and Nationality Act of 1952 undertook to codify all our national laws on immigration. This was a proper and long overdue task. But it was not just [a] housekeeping chore. In the course of the deliberation over the Act, many basic decisions about our immigration policy were made. The total racial bar against the naturalization of Japanese, Koreans and other East Asians was removed, and a minimum annual quota of one hundred was provided for each of these countries. Provision was also made to make it easier to reunite husbands and wives. Most important of all was the decision to do nothing about the national origins system.

Immigrants' Contributions

One can go on and on pointing out the contributions made by immigrants to our arts, economic growth, health, and culture in general. . . . We should continue by all means to receive these people and facilitate their entry into the United States by doing away with the inequities of the national origins quota system. America is based upon equality and fair play but our present immigration laws are contrary to the basic principles of this democracy.

A change in our immigration laws is long overdue.

John Papandreas, testimony before Congress, August 7, 1964.

The famous words of Emma Lazarus on the pedestal of the Statue of Liberty read: "Give me your tired, your poor, your huddled masses yearning to breathe free." Until 1921 this was an accurate picture of our society. Under present law it would be appropriate to add: "as long as they come from Northern Europe, are not too tired or too poor or slightly ill, never stole a loaf of bread, never joined any questionable organization, and can document their activities for the past two years."

Indefensible Racial Preference

Furthermore, the national origins quota system has strong overtones of an indefensible racial preference. It is strongly weighted toward so-called Anglo-Saxons, a phrase which one writer calls "a term of art" encompassing almost anyone from Northern and Western Europe. Sinclair Lewis described his hero, Martin Arrowsmith, this way: "a typical pure-bred-Anglo-Saxon American—which means that he was a union of German, French, Scotch-Irish, perhaps a little Spanish, conceivably of the strains lumped together as 'Jewish,' and a great deal of English, which is itself a combination of primitive Britain, Celt, Phoenician, Roman, German, Dane and Swede."

Yet, however much our present policy may be deplored, it still remains our national policy. As President Truman said when he vetoed the Immigration and Nationality Act (only to have that veto overridden): "The idea behind this discriminatory policy was, to put it boldly, that Americans with English or Irish names were better people and better citizens than Americans with Italian or Greek or Polish names. . . . Such a concept is utterly unworthy of our traditions and our ideals.". . .

There is, of course, a legitimate argument for some limitation upon immigration. We no longer need settlers for virgin lands, and our economy is expanding more slowly than in the nineteenth and early twentieth centuries. . . .

The clash of opinion arises not over the number of immigrants to be admitted, but over the test for admission—the national origins quota system. Instead of using the discriminatory test of where the immigrant was born, the reform proposals would base admission on the immigrant's possession of skills our country needs and on the humanitarian ground of reuniting families. Such legislation does not seek to make over the face of America. Immigrants would still be given tests for health, intelligence, morality and security. . . .

Religious and civic organizations, ethnic associations and newspaper editorials, citizens from every walk of life and groups of every description have expressed their support for a more rational and less prejudiced immigration law. Congressional leaders of both parties have urged the adoption of new legislation that would eliminate the most objectionable features of the [1952] McCarran-Walter Act and the nationalities quota system. . . .

A Formula for Immigration

The Presidential message to Congress of July 23, 1963, recommended that the national origins system be replaced by a formula governing immigration to the United States which takes into account: (1) the skills of the immigrant and their relationships to our needs; (2) the family relationship between immigrants and persons already here, so that the reuniting of families is encouraged; and (3) the priority of registration. Present law grants a preference to immigrants with special skills, education or training. It also grants a preference to various relatives of the United States' citizens and lawfully resident aliens. But it does so only within a national origins quota. It should be modified so that those with the greatest ability to add to the national welfare, no matter where they are born, are granted the highest priority. The next priority should go to those who seek to be reunited with their relatives. For applicants with equal claims, the earliest registrant should be the first admitted. . . .

These changes will not solve all the problems of immigration. But they will insure that progress will continue to be made toward our ideals and toward the realization of humanitarian objectives.

We must avoid what the Irish poet John Boyle O'Reilly once called

Organized charity, scrimped and iced,
In the name of a cautious, statistical Christ.

Immigration policy should be generous; it should be fair; it should be flexible. With such a policy we can turn to the world, and to our own past, with clean hands and a clear conscience. Such a policy would be but a reaffirmation of old principles. It would be an expression of our agreement with George Washington that "The bosom of America is open to receive not only the opulent and respectable stranger, but the oppressed and persecuted of all nations and religions; whom we shall welcome to a participation of all our rights and privileges, if by decency and propriety of conduct they appear to merit the enjoyment."

"Without the quota system, it is doubtful whether or not America could indefinitely maintain its traditional heritage."

National Origins Quotas Should Be Retained (1964)

Marion Moncure Duncan

Marion Moncure Duncan (1912–1978) was president general of the Daughters of the American Revolution from 1962 to 1965. DAR is a patriotic and social organization composed of female descendants of Revolutionary War veterans. The following viewpoint is taken from Duncan's 1964 testimony before Congress in which she argues against revising immigration law. Duncan asserts that national origins quotas, which since 1921 had limited immigration from places other than northern Europe, should be retained in order to maintain ethnic unity in the United States.

As you read, consider the following questions:
1. What should be the goals of immigration law, according to Duncan?
2. How are contemporary immigrants different from past immigrants, according to the author?
3. In Duncan's opinion, why are national origins quotas necessary?

Marion Moncure Duncan, statement before the U.S. House of Representatives Committee on the Judiciary, August 10, 1964.

I speak in support of maintaining the existing provisions of the Immigration and Nationality Act of 1952, especially the national origins quota system. . . .

I speak not as a specialist or authority in a particular field. Rather, the focus is that of attempting to present to you and ask your consideration of the conscientious convictions of an organization keenly and, more importantly, actively interested in this subject almost since its own inception nearly three-quarters of a century ago. . . .

The DAR is not taking a stand against immigration per se. Any inference in that direction is in error and completely false. DAR, as a national organization, is among the foremost "to extend a helping hand" to immigrants admitted on an intelligent, orderly, equitable basis such as is allowed under the current Immigration and Nationality Act of 1952. If, from time to time, there be need for change or adjustment, it should be provided through logical, deliberate amendment, still retaining the national origins quota system and other vitally basic, protective features of the law. These constitute a first line of defense in perpetuating and maintaining our institutions of freedom and the American way of life. To discard them would endanger both.

From the point that immigration is definitely a matter of national welfare and security, it is imperative that a logical and rational method of governing and administering same be maintained. The [1952] Walter-McCarran Act has done and will continue equitably to accomplish just this. It denies no nation a quota, but it does provide a reasonable, orderly, mathematical formula (based, of course, upon the 1920 census figures) which is devoid of the political pressure which could inevitably be expected to beset any commission authorized to reapportion unused quotas as proposed in the legislation before you.

The 1952 Immigration Act

By way of background: What prompted passage of the Immigration-Nationality Act of 1952? It will be recalled that this was the product of a tedious, comprehensive study of nearly 5 years' duration, covering some 200 laws on selective immigration, special orders and exclusions, and spanned the period from passage of the first quota law by Congress in 1924. This law codified and coordinated all existing immigration, nationality, and deportation laws.

Despite repeated efforts to weaken, circumvent and bypass this protective legislation, its soundness has been demonstrated over the period it has been in operation.

The United States Must Be Selective

We will gain neither respect, gratitude, nor love from other nations by making our homes their doormat. Nations, like men, must be reasonably selective about whom they adopt into the bosom of their family. . . .

We cannot maintain our priceless heritage of individual liberty as outlined in the three classic cornerstones of our Republic; in the Declaration of Independence, our Federal and State Constitutions, and our Bill of Rights, if we permit our already overpacked "melting pot," to be inundated from the world's most deprived areas; or if we break down those barriers which now permit us to screen out those who neither know, nor appreciate, the value of American institutions or the aims of our great country.

Myra C. Hacker, statement before Congress, August 11, 1964.

It embodies the following important features—all in the best interest of our constitutional republic:

(*a*) Recognizing the cultural identity and historic population basis of this Nation, it officially preserved the national origin quota system as the basis for immigration, wisely giving preference to those nations whose composite culture—Anglo-Saxon from northern and western European countries—has been responsible for and actually produced the American heritage as we know it today.

(*b*) It abolished certain discriminatory provisions in our immigration laws—those against sexes and persons of Asiatic origin.

(*c*) "Quality versus quantity" preference for skilled aliens was provided, as well as broadened classifications for non-quota immigrants. No nation or race is listed ineligible for immigration and naturalization, although the acknowledged purpose is to preserve this country's culture, free institutions, free enterprise economy and racial complex, yes, and likely even language. Ready assimilability of the majority of immigrants is a prime factor.

(*d*) It provides the U.S. Immigration Department with needed authority to cope with subversive aliens by strengthening security provisions.

Perhaps the sentiment and deep concern of the DAR relative to the matter of immigration and its appeal for retention of the present law is best expressed by excerpting salient points from recent resolutions on the subject:

(1) For building unity and cohesiveness among American citizens, whose social, economic and spiritual mind has been and is under increasing pressures and conflicts, wise and comprehensive steps must be taken.

(2) For the protection and interest of all citizens from foreign elements imbued with ideologies wholly at variance with our republican form of government should be excluded.

On basis of FBI [Federal Bureau of Investigation] analysis statistics and information available through investigation by the House Un-American Activities Committee, loopholes through which thousands of criminal aliens may enter this country constitute a continuing threat for the safety of American institutions.

(3) Since it is a recognized fact that free migration allowing unhampered movement of agents is necessary for triumph of either a world socialist state or international communism as a world conspiracy, this would explain the motivation on the part of enemies of this country for concentrated effort to undermine the existing immigration law.

(4) Admittedly, major problems confronting the Nation and threatening its national economy are unemployment, housing, education, security, population explosion, and other domestic problems such as juvenile delinquency, crime, and racial tensions. This is borne out by numerous statistics and the current Federal war on poverty effort. In view of this, revisions as per proposed new quotas to greatly increase the number of immigrants would be a threat to the security and well-being of this Nation, especially in face of the cold war inasmuch as it would be impossible to obtain adequate security checks on immigrants from satellite Communist-controlled countries.

In summation: A comparative study would indicate increased aggravation of existing problems and unfavorable repercussions on all facets of our economy such as employment, housing, education, welfare, health, and national security, offering additional threats to the American heritage—cultural, social, and ethnic traditions. . . .

The Difference Between Then and Now

While DAR would be the first to admit the importance of immigrants to America, its membership ties linking directly with the first waves of immigrants to these shores, it would seem well, however, to point out a "then and now" difference factor currently exists attributable to time and circumstance—no uncomplimentary inference therein. A common desire shared by immigrants of all time to America has been the seeking of freedom or the escape from tyranny. But in the early days, say the first 150 years, it is noteworthy that those who came shared common Anglo-Saxon bonds and arrived with the full knowledge and intent of founders or pioneers who knew there was a wilderness to conquer and a nation to build. Their coming indicated a willingness to make a contribution and assume such a role. In the intervening years, many fine, high-caliber immigrants, and I know some at personal sacrifice, following ideals in which they believed, have likewise come to America imbued with a constructive desire to produce and add to the glory of their new homeland. They, however, have come to a nation already established with cultural patterns set and traditions already rooted.

Further, in recent years, en masse refugee movements, though responding to the very same ideal which is America, have been motivated primarily by escape. This has had a tendency possibly to dim individual purpose and dedication and possibly project beyond other considerations, the available benefits to be secured as an American citizen.

Abandonment of the national origins system would drastically alter the source of our immigration. Any change would not take into consideration that those whose background and heritage most closely resemble our own are most readily assimilable.

In testimony before you, this point was touched upon by

a high official when he said, "To apply the new principle rigidly would result, after a few years, in eliminating immigration from these countries almost entirely." Admittedly such a situation would be undesirable. A strict first-come, first-served basis of allocating visa quotas as proposed would create certain problems in countries of northern and western Europe, and could ultimately dry up influx from that area.

The Quota System Is Fair

The fact is that the national origins quota system does not predicate the quotas upon the race, culture, morality, intelligence, health, physical attributes, or any other characteristics of the people in any foreign country.

The quotas are based upon our own people. The national origins system is like a mirror held up before the American people and reflecting the proportions of their various foreign national origins.

Assertions by critics that the national origins system is in some way discriminatory or establishes the principle that some foreign nations or ethnic groups are defined as "superior" or "inferior" are entirely without foundation.

National origins simply attempts to have immigration into the United States conform in composition to our own people.

John B. Trevor Jr., testimony before Congress, May 20, 1965.

Going a step further, would not the abolishment of the national origin quota system work a hardship and possibly result in actual discrimination against the very nations who supplied the people who now comprises the majority of our historic population mixture? Further, such a change in our existing laws would appear to be an outright accommodation to the heaviest population explosions throughout the world—India, Asia, and Africa. Certainly these countries could naturally be expected to take full advantage of such an increased quota opportunity.

Is it, therefore, desirable or in the best interest to assign possible 10-percent quotas to say proliferating African nations to the end that our own internal problems become manifold? America, as all other nations, is concerned over rapid population growth of this era. Staggering statistics are readily available on every hand.

Immigration Is a Privilege

Attention is called to the fact that immigration is not an alien's right; it is a privilege. With privilege comes its hand-maiden responsibility. Before tampering with the present immigration law, much less destroying its basic principles, due regard must also be given to our own unemployment situation. No less an authority than the late President John F. Kennedy, who was for this bill, stated on March 3, 1963, that we had 5 million unemployed and 2 million people displaced each year by advancing technology and automation.

Irrespective of recent and reoccurring reports on unemployment showing temporary increases or decreases, the fact is, it remains a matter of economic concern. Latest figures available as of June 1964 indicate 4.7 million or 5.3 percent.

In view of this, it would seem highly incongruent if not outright incredible to find ourselves in a situation, on the one hand, waging war on poverty and unemployment at home, while on the other hand, simultaneously and indiscriminately letting down immigration bars to those abroad. Not only employment alone but mental health and retardation problems could greatly increase. Another source of concern to the heavy laden taxpayer to whom already the national debt figure is astronomical.

It is asserted that our economy will get three consumers for every worker admitted and that our economy generates jobs at a rate better than one for every three consumers. Why, then, are we presently plagued with unemployment? And how is it possible to guarantee that these new immigrants will "fill jobs that are going begging because there are not enough skilled workers in our economy who have the needed skills?" Are there enough such jobs going begging to justify destroying an immigration law which has been described as our first line of defense?

Rightly, it would seem U.S. citizens should have first claim on jobs and housing in this country. With manpower available and the recent emphasis on expanded educational facilities, why is not definite concentrated effort made to provide and accelerate vocational and special skill training for the many who either through disinclination, native inability or otherwise are not qualified potentials for schooling in the field of science, medicine, law, or other such professions?

The Need for National Quotas

Without the quota system, it is doubtful whether or not America could indefinitely maintain its traditional heritage: Economic, cultural, social, ethnic, or even language.

Free institutions as we have known them would stand to undergo radical change if the proposal to permit reapportionment of unused quotas is also adopted. It is felt reassignment of unused quotas would be as damaging to the basic principles of the Immigration and Nationality Act as repeal of the national origins system itself. . . .

The National Society, Daughters of the American Revolution, which initially supported the Walter-McCarran bill when it was introduced and has continuously done so since, wishes again to officially reaffirm its support of the existing law, firmly believing that the present Immigration and Nationality Act of 1952 not only safeguards our constitutional Republic and perpetuates our American heritage, but by maintaining its established standards, that it actually protects the naturalized American on a par with the native born, and as well offers encouragement to desirable immigrants to become future American citizens. Any breakdown in this system would be an open invitation to Communist infiltration. Likewise, a poor law, newly enacted, and improperly administered, could provide the same opportunity to the detriment, if not the actual downfall, of our country.

The well-intentioned, humanitarian plea that America's unrestricted assumption of the overpopulous, troubled, ailing people of the world within our own borders is unrealistic, impractical, and if done in excess could spell economic bankruptcy for our people from point of both employment and overladen taxes to say nothing of a collapse of morale and spiritual values if nonassimilable aliens of dissimilar ethnic background and culture by wholesale and indiscriminate transporting en masse overturn the balance of our national character.

In connection with the liberalization proposals, it would seem timely to refer to the words of Senator Patrick Mc-

Carran, who, when he presented the bill, warned:

> If the enemies of this legislation succeed in riddling it to pieces, or in amending it beyond recognition, they will have contributed more to promote this Nation's downfall than any other group since we achieved our independence as a nation.

Somewhat the same sentiment was expressed by Abraham Lincoln, who admonished:

> You cannot strengthen the weak by weakening the strong; and you cannot help men permanently by doing for them what they could and should do for themselves.

Many inspiring words have been written of America. I would conclude with those of the late historian, James Truslow Adams:

> America's greatest contribution to the world has been that of the American dream, the dream of a land where life shall be richer, fuller, and better, with opportunity for every person according to his ability and achievement.

The question is: Can it continue so if, through reckless abandon, the United States becomes mired, causing the country to lose its image as the land of opportunity, the home of the free? Ours is the responsibility to maintain and preserve it for the future.

Is Immigration a Serious Problem?

Chapter Preface

The United States has long been known as a country of immigrants. Yet more than two hundred years after the nation's founding, policymakers cannot agree on whether America should continue to accept foreign-born citizens. Some are particularly concerned about the recent wave of Hispanic and Asian immigrants and the relatively high birthrates among these groups. The U.S. Census Bureau predicts that by the year 2050, the Latino population will increase from 10 percent to 25 percent, while the Asian population will increase from 3 percent to 8 percent. Although the black American population will remain relatively stable at 14 percent, the percentage of native-born whites will decrease from 74 percent to 53 percent. By 2010, several states will no longer have a "majority" ethnic group—that is, a group that comprises more than 50 percent of the population.

Some analysts fear that such dramatic changes in America's ethnic makeup threaten national unity. As the U.S. population becomes more diverse, interethnic tensions can increase as immigrants and native-born Americans compete for jobs, living space, and political power, contends *Washington Post* staff writer William Booth. Moreover, many immigrants and their descendants cling to their heritage and resist identifying themselves as American, Booth maintains. In the end, he believes, the nation could "fracture into many separate, disconnected communities with no shared sense of commonality or purpose. Or perhaps it will evolve into something in between, a pluralistic society that will hold on to some core ideas about citizenship or capitalism, but with little meaningful interaction among groups."

Supporters of immigration, however, assert that immigrants are a source of strength for America. While an influx of new residents from different cultures presents some challenges, the United States has always been energized by its immigrant populations, proponents contend. In a 1998 commencement address at Portland State University, then-President Bill Clinton voiced support for immigrants, including those from Asia and Latin America: "America has constantly drawn strength and spirit from wave after wave of immigrants. . . . They have proved to be the most restless, the most adventurous, the most innovative, the most industrious of people. Bearing different memories, honoring different heritages, they have strengthened our economy, enriched our culture, renewed our promise of freedom and opportunity for all." Americans need to cultivate their capacity for humor, empathy, and forbearance when facing the challenges posed by immigration, advocates maintain.

The vision of America as a land of freedom and opportunity will continue to encourage people from around the world to come to the United States. The authors in the following chapter examine whether these newcomers are a boon or a burden to their new homeland.

"We face a . . . serious threat to the very survival of our civilization."

Immigration Is Harming American Culture

Lawrence Auster

Lawrence Auster is the author of *The Path to National Suicide: An Essay on Immigration and Multiculturalism* and *Huddled Cliches: Exposing the Fraudulent Arguments That Have Opened America's Borders to the World.* In the following viewpoint, Auster contends that mass immigration poses a significant threat to American culture. The influx of immigrants from non-Western nations is particularly dangerous, Auster writes, because the beliefs of these cultures often conflict with American values and customs. Moreover, Americans themselves contribute to the immigrant threat when they uphold the principle of nondiscrimination toward other cultures. Widely diverse cultures cannot coexist within the same borders, Auster maintains. Americans must come to see themselves as a distinct people and drastically reduce immigration if they wish to preserve their nation.

As you read, consider the following questions:
1. In Auster's view, what are some specific examples of the problems posed by immigration?
2. According to the author, how has President George W. Bush contributed to the immigrant threat?
3. In what way does multiculturalism oppose God's design, in Auster's opinion?

Lawrence Auster, "Mass Immigration: Its Effect on Our Culture," *The Social Contract*, vol. XII, Spring 2002, pp. 215–18. Copyright © 2002 by Lawrence Auster. Reproduced by permission.

The problem of immigration and the changes it is causing in our culture can be approached from many different angles. We could speak about the redefinition of America as a multicultural society instead of as a nation; or the permanent establishment of affirmative action programs for immigrants based on their race; or the town in Texas that declared Spanish its official language; or the thousands of Hispanics at an international soccer match in Los Angeles who booed and threw garbage at the *American* team; or the decline in educational and environmental standards in areas dominated by Hispanics; or the Hmong people from Laos who bring shamans and witch doctors into hospital rooms; or the customs of voodoo and animal sacrifice and forced marriage and female genital mutilation that have been imported into this country by recent immigrants; or the pushing aside of Christianity in our public life to give equal respect to non-Western religions; or the evisceration of American history in our schools because our white-majority American past is no longer seen as representative of our newly diverse population; or the vast numbers of Muslims established in cities throughout this country who sympathize with the Muslim terrorists and dream of turning America into an Islamic state; or *our own leaders* who, even *after* the September 11, 2001, [terrorist attacks] keep telling us that the Muslims are all patriotic and tolerant, keep warning *us* against our supposed anti-Muslim bigotry, and continue letting thousands of people from terror supporting countries to immigrate into America.

At bottom, each of these phenomena and many more like them are happening for one reason and one reason only—the 1965 Immigration Act which opened U.S. immigration on an equal basis to every country in the world, rather than, as in the past, favoring our historic source nations of Europe. Of course many of the recent immigrants from non-European countries have fitted into America and made good contributions here. It is the unprecedented scale of this diverse immigration that is the problem.

I could easily devote the rest of this article to making a detailed case that the post-1965 immigration is indeed changing our culture in negative ways. But here I want to ask a different question: Why have *we Americans* allowed this to oc-cur? Why are we *continuing* to let it happen? And why, even when we gripe and complain about some aspects of it, do we feel *helpless* to do anything to stop it?

Mainstream Beliefs

Many have argued, most recently [syndicated columnist] Patrick Buchanan, that these things are happening because of the cultural left that hates America and wants to destroy it. There is no doubt that the cultural left hates America and wants to destroy it; and there is also no doubt that the left see mass immigration from Third-World countries as a handy way of achieving that. But that argument leaves unanswered a more disturbing question—why has there been no significant opposition to this leftist agenda? Presumably, the Republican party does not hate America and want to destroy it. Presumably, the conservative movement does not hate America and want to destroy it. Presumably conservative Protestants and parents' groups that have fought against Whole Language teaching and homosexual indoctrination in the schools do not hate America and want to destroy it. Yet nowhere among these legions of mainstream conservatives and the organizations that represent them have there been any serious calls to reduce this immigration from the non-Western world and the inevitable cultural transformations it is bringing.

Nor is the fear of political correctness (PC) an adequate explanation for this conservative surrender. Whatever the power of PC in our society, it cannot account for the fact that tens of millions of mainstream conservatives ranging from [radio personality] Rush Limbaugh fans to conserva-tive evangelicals either support the current immigration pol-icy or fail to speak up against it—even in the relative privacy and safety of their own organizations.

We are thus left with a remarkable paradox—that the pa-triotic and Christian Right supports exactly the same immi-gration policy that is supported by the anti-American, athe-istic left—an immigration policy, moreover, that spells the permanent eclipse of the Republican party and the victory of big government, since most of the recent immigrants vote Democratic.

Indeed, our conservative Christian President, when he's not busy embracing so-called "moderate" Muslim leaders who are allies of terrorists, wants to expand Third-World immigration even further. But that's not all. Unlike Republicans in the past such as Ronald Reagan, who supported Third-World immigration on the hopeful if naive assumption that the immigrants were all assimilating, President George W. Bush actively promotes the growth and development of foreign languages and unassimilated foreign cultures in this country. In a speech in Miami, Florida, during the 2000 campaign, he celebrated the fact that American cities are becoming culturally and linguistically like Latin American cities:

> We are now one of the largest Spanish-speaking nations in the world. We're a major source of Latin music, journalism and culture. . . . Just go to Miami, or San Antonio, Los Angeles, Chicago or West New York, New Jersey . . . and close your eyes and listen. You could just as easily be in Santo Domingo or Santiago, or San Miguel de Allende. . . . For years our nation has debated this change—some have praised it and others have resented it. *By nominating me, my party has made a choice to welcome the new America.*

As president, Mr. Bush has not only left in place Bill Clinton's executive order requiring government services to be provided in foreign languages, he has started his own bilingual tradition, delivering a Spanish version of his weekly national radio address. Even the White House Web site is now bilingual, with a link accompanying each of the president's speeches that says *"En Español"* and points to a Spanish translation of the speech.

Yet, with the exception of one or two conservative columnists, these steps toward the establishment of Spanish as a quasi-official public language in this country have been met with complete silence on the right, even though opposition to bilingualism used to command automatic agreement among conservatives. If conservatives are no longer willing to utter a peep of protest in defense of something so fundamental to America as our national language, is there anything else about our historic culture they will defend, once it has been abandoned by a Republican president?

What all of this suggests is that mass immigration and the

resulting multiculturalism are not—as many immigration restrictionists tend to believe—simply being imposed on us by the anti-American left. Rather, these destructive phenomena stem from *mainstream beliefs* that are shared by most Americans, particularly by conservatives. Of course economic and political forces, and the birthrate factor, are pushing this process in a variety of ways, but on the deepest level the cause is not material, it is philosophical and spiritual. The reason Americans cannot effectively oppose the transformation of our culture is that they subscribe to the belief system that has led to it.

The Problem with Individualism

What is that belief system? At its core, it is the quintessentially American notion that everyone is the same under the skin—that people should only be seen as individuals, with no reference to their historic culture, their ethnicity, their religion, their race. Now there is a great truth in the idea of a common human essence transcending our material differences. But if it is taken to be literally true in all circumstances and turned into an ideological dogma, it leads to the expectation that all people from every background and in whatever numbers can assimilate equally well into America.

This explains why patriotic conservatives acquiesce in a policy that is so obviously dividing and weakening our nation. Since the end of World War II, and especially since the 1960s, conservatives have tended to define America not in terms of its historic civilization and peoplehood, but almost exclusively in terms of the *individual*—the individual under God and the individual as an economic actor. For modern conservatives, what makes America is not any inherited cultural tradition from our past, but our belief in the timeless, universal, God-granted right of all persons in the world to be free and to improve their own lives. Therefore conservatives don't believe there can be any moral basis to make distinctions among prospective immigrants based on their culture.

We cannot say, for example, that a shaman-following Laotian tribesman, or a Pakistani who believes in forced marriage, is less suited for membership in our society than an Italian Catholic or a Scots-Irish Presbyterian. And we can't make such distinctions because, from the point of view of pure individualism, our inherited culture does not reflect any inherent or higher truth, and therefore cannot be the object of our love and protection. The only value that reflects higher truth and is deserving of our energetic defense is the freedom and sacredness of each individual. In practical terms this translates into the equal right of all individuals to make their own choices and pursue their own dreams, even if we are speaking of tens of millions of people from alien cultures whose exercise of *their* individual right to come to America will mean the destruction of *our* cultural goods.

Ethnic Divides

Native-born white liberals use "diversity" to justify mass immigration beyond the ability of the melting pot to assimilate. But the unassimilated immigrants are not as tolerant of diversity as their white liberal spokespersons. Mario Obledo, co-founder of the Mexican American Legal Defense Fund, said on a radio program that Hispanics are going to take over all the political institutions of California and anyone who does not like it should leave.

In Dearborn, Michigan, school fights have erupted between Arabs and non-Arabs, in New Jersey between Koreans and non-Koreans, in Maryland communities between Russian immigrants and native-born U.S. citizens, in Lexington, Kentucky, between blacks and Hispanics.

Paul Craig Roberts, syndicated column, June 21, 1999.

In theory, multiculturalism is the opposite of liberal individualism. In practice it is the direct result of pursuing liberal individualism to its logical extreme. The 1965 Immigration Act was not about multiculturalism. No lawmaker said in 1965: Hey, we *need* Third-World cultures, we *need* female genital mutilation in our country, we *need* Shiite Islam and Wahabbi Islam to fulfill the meaning of America. The 1965 legislators voted to open our borders to the world, not because of a belief in the equal value of all cultures, but because of a belief in the equal rights of all individuals; the single comment most frequently heard in the Congressional debate was that prospective immigrants should be chosen solely on the basis of their "individual worth." But this noble-sounding sentiment was an illusion, because, in the real world, most of the people admitted into America under the new law did not come just as individuals. They came as part of the largest mass migration in history, consisting largely of family chain migration, and inevitably brought their cultures with them.

Defining America Out of Existence

Thus, in passing the 1965 Immigration Act, we did two fateful things. We announced that we had no culture of our own except for the principle of non-discrimination toward people of *other* cultures—*and* we began admitting millions of people from those other cultures. We started letting in all these other cultures at the very moment that we had *defined our own culture out of existence.*

This delusional act led to the next stage of our self-undoing. In the late 1970s and 1980s, we began waking up to the fact that those other cultures were here, that they were very different from our own, and that they were demanding to be recognized and given rights as cultures. But at that point, what basis did we have to resist those demands? We had already said that the only thing that defines us as a people is non-discrimination toward other peoples; we thus had no justification for saying that maybe it's not such a great idea to import people adhering to radical Islam or Mexican nationalism into the United States. Having cast aside our own culture, we had no choice but to yield, step by step, to the elevation of other cultures. This is how America, through an indiscriminate and unqualified belief in individualism, ended up surrendering to its opposite—to multiculturalism.

Cultural Differences Matter

What has been said up to this point will offend many conservatives, particularly Christians. For one thing, the Christian church consists of people of every culture and race, so why can't a nation? The answer is that the church is a heavenly organization, it is not responsible, as a nation is, for the defense and preservation of a particular earthly society. Mexico and Nigeria, for example, are largely Christian, but in cultural terms are radically different from the United States.

To believe that all peoples on earth should join our country is the very idea that God rejected at the tower of Babel. God said he did not want all men to be united in one society, because that would glorify human power. If I may presume to say so, God had a more modest idea of human life on earth. He wanted men to live in distinct societies, each speaking its own tongue, developing its own culture, and expressing God in its own way. This is the true diversity of cultures that constitutes mankind, not the false diversity that results from eliminating borders and coercively mixing everyone together, which destroys each country's distinctive character. Consider how today's multicultural London has lost much of its Englishness, and increasingly resembles multicultural New York.

So I would respectfully suggest that when Christians translate the spiritual idea of the unity of people under God into the political ideology that people from all cultures should be allowed to come en masse to America and other Western countries, that is not the traditional teaching of the Christian church, that is a modern liberal idea, that is the *Religion of Man*, which has been infused into the Christian church over the past fifty years.

But if this is the case, how can we reconcile our spiritual unity as human beings under God with our actual cultural differences? The answer is that in individual and private relationships, people of different backgrounds can relate to each other as individuals, without discrimination of culture and ethnicity. But on the group level, on the level of entire peoples and nations and mass migrations, cultural differences do matter very much and cannot be safely ignored.

Thinking and Acting Anew

It would therefore be a tragic error to limit our thinking about immigration to technical matters such as law enforcement against illegal aliens and security measures against terrorists, as vitally important as those things are. Beyond the immediate threat of mass physical destruction, we face a more subtle but no less serious threat to the very survival of our civilization. As [author and historian] Daniel Pipes writes in *Commentary:* "To me, the current wave of militant Islamic violence against the United States, however dangerous, is ultimately less consequential than the non-violent effort to transform it through immigration, natural reproduction, and conversion."

Of course I agree with Mr. Pipes. But, as I've tried to demonstrate, we cannot hope to stop or significantly slow that immigration unless we abandon this contemporary idea that America is defined by *nothing* except individual freedom and opportunity—the idea that America has no particular culture of its own that is worth preserving. Rethinking these beliefs and rewriting our immigration laws accordingly will not be easy, but if we fail to make the attempt, we will simply continue sliding, slowly but surely, toward the dissolution of our culture and our country.

"Immigration [can help] us become a stronger nation . . . in the global competition of civilizations."

Immigration Is Good for American Culture

Ben Wattenberg

Immigration benefits America, argues Ben Wattenberg in the following viewpoint. The birth rate in the United States and other Western nations has been decreasing, he points out. Lower populations in the Western world could make it more difficult for beneficial Western values—such as pluralism, democracy, and individual liberty—to be globally influential. But if the United States continues to take in immigrants—including immigrants from third world and non-Western nations—its population will grow and help to fortify American power and influence around the world. Wattenberg is a senior fellow at the American Enterprise Institute, a conservative think tank. He is also the author of *The Birth Dearth* and *Survival 101.*

As you read, consider the following questions:
1. What is absurd about rigid racial definitions, in Wattenberg's opinion?
2. According to the author, what percentage of the population was foreign born in 1999?
3. In the year 2000, modern Western nations made up what fraction of the global population, according to Wattenberg?

Ben Wattenberg, "Immigration: A Cause of the Clash of Civilizations . . . or a Solution to It?" *The American Enterprise*, vol. 13, March 2002, pp. 22–24.

M any leading thinkers tell us we are now in a culture clash that will determine the course of history, that today's war is for Western civilization itself. There is a demographic dimension to this "clash of civilizations." While certain of today's demographic signals bode well for America, some look very bad. If we are to assess America's future prospects, we must start by asking. "Who are we?" "Who will we be?" and "How will we relate to the rest of the world?" The answers all involve immigration.

As data from the 2000 census trickled out, one item hit the headline jackpot. By the year 2050, we were told, America would be "majority non-white." The census count showed more Hispanics in America than had been expected, making them "America's largest minority." When blacks, Asians, and Native Americans are added to the Hispanic total, the "non-white" population emerges as a large minority, on the way to becoming a small majority around the middle of the twenty-first century.

The first thing worth noting is that these rigid racial definitions are absurd. The whole concept of race as a biological category is becoming ever-more dubious in America. Consider:

Under the Bill Clinton administration's census rules, any American who checks both the black and white boxes on the form inquiring about "race" is counted as black, even if his heritage is, say, one eighth black and seven eighths white. In effect, this enshrines the infamous segregationist view that one drop of black blood makes a person black.

Although most Americans of Hispanic heritage declare themselves "white," they are often inferentially counted as non-white, as in the erroneous *New York Times* headline which recently declared: "Census Confirms Whites Now a Minority" in California.

If those of Hispanic descent, hailing originally from about 40 nations, are counted as a minority, why aren't those of Eastern European descent, coming from about 10 nations, also counted as a minority? (In which case the Eastern European "minority" would be larger than the Hispanic minority.)

But within this jumble of numbers there lies a central truth: America is becoming a universal nation, with significant representation of nearly all human hues, creeds, ethnicities, and national ancestries. Continued moderate immigration will make us an even more universal nation as time goes on. And this process may well play a serious role in determining the outcome of the contest of civilizations taking place across the globe.

And current immigration rates are moderate, even though America admitted more legal immigrants from 1991 to 2000 than in any previous decade—between 10 and 11 million. The highest previous decade was 1901–1910, when 8.8 million people arrived. In addition, each decade now, several million illegal immigrants enter the U.S., thanks partly to ease of transportation.

Immigrants Will Not "Swamp" America

Critics like Pat Buchanan say that absorbing all those immigrants will "swamp" the American culture and bring Third World chaos inside our borders. I disagree. Keep in mind: Those 8.8 million immigrants who arrived in the U.S. between 1901 and 1910 increased the total American population by 1 percent per year. (Our numbers grew from 76 million to 92 million during that decade.) In our most recent decade, on the other hand, the 10 million legal immigrants represented annual growth of only 0.36 percent (as the U.S. went from 249 million to 281 million).

Overall, nearly 15 percent of Americans were foreign-born in 1910. In 1999, our foreign-born were about 10 percent of our total. (In 1970, the foreign-born portion of our population was down to about 5 percent. Most of the rebound resulted from a more liberal immigration law enacted in 1965.) Or look at the "foreign stock" data. These figures combine Americans born in foreign lands and their offspring, even if those children have only one foreign-born parent. Today, America's "foreign stock" amounts to 21 percent of the population and heading up. But in 1910, the comparable figure was 34 percent—one third of the entire country—and the heavens did not collapse.

We can take in more immigrants, if we want to. Should we?

Return to the idea that immigrants could swamp American culture. If that is true, we clearly should not increase our intake. But what if instead of swamping us, immigration helps us become a stronger nation and a swamper of others in the global competition of civilizations?

Immigration is now what keeps America growing. According to the U.N., the typical American woman today bears an average of 1.93 children over the course of her childbearing years. That is mildly below the 2.1 "replacement" rate required to keep a population stable over time, absent immigration. The "medium variant" of the most recent Census Bureau projections posits that the U.S. population will grow from 281 million in 2000 to 397 million in 2050 with expected immigration, but only to 328 million should we choose a path of zero immigration. That is a difference of a population growth of 47 million versus 116 million. (The 47 million rise is due mostly to demographic momentum from previous higher birthrates.) If we have zero immigration with today's low birthrates indefinitely, the American population would eventually begin to shrink, albeit slowly.

Good for America

I believe new immigrants are good for America. They are revitalizing our cities. They are building our new economy. They are strengthening our ties to the global economy, just as earlier waves of immigrants settled on the new frontier and powered the Industrial Revolution. They are energizing our culture and broadening our vision of the world. They are renewing our most basic values and reminding us all of what it truly means to be an American.

Bill Clinton, Commencement Address at Portland State University, June 13, 1998.

Is more population good for America? When it comes to potential global power and influence, numbers can matter a great deal. Taxpayers, many of them, pay for a fleet of aircraft carriers. And on the economic side it is better to have a customer boom than a customer bust. (It may well be that Japan's stagnant demography is one cause of its decade-long slump.) The environmental case could be debated all day long, but remember that an immigrant does not add to the global population—he merely moves from one spot on the planet to another.

But will the current crop of immigrants acculturate? Immigrants to America always have. Some critics, like Mr. Buchanan, claim that this time, it's different. Mexicans seem to draw his particular ire, probably because they are currently our largest single source of immigration.

Yet only about a fifth (22 percent) of legal immigrants to America currently come from Mexico. Adding illegal immigrants might boost the figure to 30 percent, but the proportion of Mexican immigrants will almost surely shrink over time. Mexican fertility has diminished from 6.5 children per woman 30 years ago to 2.5 children now, and continues to fall. If high immigration continues under such circumstances, Mexico will run out of Mexicans.

California hosts a wide variety of immigrant groups in addition to Mexicans. And the children and grandchildren of Koreans, Chinese, Khmer, Russian Jews, Iranians, and Thai (to name a few) will speak English, not Spanish. Even among Mexican-Americans, many second- and third-generation offspring speak no Spanish at all, often to the dismay of their elders (a familiar American story).

Michael Barone's book *The New Americans* theorizes that Mexican immigrants are following roughly the same course of earlier Italian and Irish immigrants. Noel Ignatiev's book *How the Irish Became White* notes that it took a hundred years until Irish-Americans (who were routinely characterized as drunken "gorillas") reached full income parity with the rest of America.

California has repealed its bilingual education programs. Nearly half of Latino voters supported the proposition, even though it was demonized by opponents as being anti-Hispanic. Latina mothers reportedly tell their children, with no intent to disparage the Spanish language, that "Spanish is the language of busboys"—stressing that in America you have to speak English to get ahead.

Changing Views

The huge immigration wave at the dawn of the twentieth century undeniably brought tumult to America. Many early social scientists promoted theories of what is now called "scientific racism," which "proved" that persons from Northwest Europe were biologically superior. The new immigrants—Jews, Poles, and Italians—were considered racially apart and far down the totem pole of human character and intelligence. Blacks and Asians were hardly worth measuring. The immigration wave sparked a resurgence of the Ku Klux Klan (KKK), peaking in the early 1920s. At that time, the biggest KKK state was not in the South; it was Indiana, where Catholics, Jews, and immigrants, as well as blacks, were targets.

Francis Walker, superintendent of the U.S. Bureau of the Census in the late 1890s, and later president of Massachusetts Institute of Technology (MIT), wrote in 1896 that "The entrance of such vast masses of peasantry degraded below our utmost conceptions is a matter which no intelligent patriot can look upon without the gravest apprehension and alarm. They are beaten men from beaten races. They have none of the ideas and aptitudes such as belong to those who were descended from the tribes that met under the oak trees of old Germany to make laws and choose chiefs." (Sorry, Francis, but Germany did not have a good twentieth century.)

Fast-forward to the present. By high margins, Americans now tell pollsters it was a very good thing that Poles, Italians, and Jews emigrated to America. Once again, it's the newcomers who are viewed with suspicion. This time, it's the Mexicans, Filipinos, and people from the Caribbean who make Americans nervous. But such views change over time. The newer immigrant groups are typically more popular now than they were even a decade ago.

Look at the high rates of intermarriage. Most Americans have long since lost their qualms about marriage between people of different European ethnicities. That is spreading across new boundaries. In 1990, 64 percent of Asian Americans married outside their heritage, as did 37 percent of Hispanics. Black-white intermarriage is much lower, but it climbed from 3 percent in 1980 to 9 percent in 1998. (One reason to do away with the race question on the census is that within a few decades we won't be able to know who's what.)

Can the West, led by America, prevail in a world full of sometimes unfriendly neighbors? Substantial numbers of people are necessary (though not sufficient) for a country, or a civilization, to be globally influential. Will America and its Western allies have enough people to keep their ideas and principles alive?

On the surface, it doesn't look good. In 1986, I wrote a book called *The Birth Dearth*. My thesis was that birth rates in developed parts of the world—Europe, North America, Australia, and Japan, nations where liberal Western values are rooted—had sunk so low that there was danger ahead. At that time, women in those modern countries were bearing a lifetime average of 1.83 children, the lowest rate ever absent war, famine, economic depression, or epidemic illness. It was, in fact, 15 percent below the longterm population replacement level.

Those trendlines have now plummeted even further. Today, the fertility rate in the modern countries averages 1.5 children per woman, 28 percent below the replacement level. The European rate, astonishingly, is 1.34 children per woman—radically below replacement level. The Japanese rate is similar. The United States is the exceptional country in the current demographic scene.

As a whole, the nations of the Western world will soon be less populous, and a substantially smaller fraction of the world population. Demographer Samuel Preston estimates that even if European fertility rates jump back to replacement level immediately (which won't happen) the continent would still lose 100 million people by 2060. Should the rate not level off fairly soon, the ramifications are incalculable, or, as the Italian demographer Antonio Golini likes to mutter at demographic meetings, "unsustainable . . . unsustainable." (Shockingly, the current Italian fertility rate is 1.2 children per woman, and it has been at or below 1.5 for 20 years—a full generation.)

The modern countries of the world, the bearers of Western civilization, made up one third of the global population in 1950, and one fifth in 2000, and are projected to represent one eighth by 2050. If we end up in a world with nine competing civilizations, as [political scientist] Samuel Huntington maintains, this will make it that much harder for Western values to prevail in the cultural and political arenas.

The good news is that fertility rates have also plunged in the less developed countries—from 6 children in 1970 to 2.9 today. By the middle to end of [the twenty-first] century, there should be a rough global convergence of fertility rates and population growth.

America Needs Immigrants

Since [the September 11, 2001, terrorist attacks on America] immigration has gotten bad press in America. The terrorist villains, indeed, were foreigners. Not only in the U.S. but in many other nations as well, governments are suddenly cracking down on illegal entry. This is understandable for the moment. But an enduring turn away from legal immigration would be foolhardy for America and its allies.

If America doesn't continue to take in immigrants, it won't continue to grow in the long run. If the Europeans and Japanese don't start to accept more immigrants they will evaporate. Who will empty the bedpans in Italy's retirement homes? The only major pool of immigrants available to Western countries hails from the less developed world, i.e. non-white, and non-Western countries.

The West as a whole is in a deep demographic ditch. Accordingly, Western countries should try to make it easier for couples who want to have children. In America, the advent of tax credits for children (which went from zero to $1,000 per child per year over the last decade) is a small step in the direction of fertility reflation. Some European nations are enacting similar pro-natal policies. But their fertility rates are so low, and their economies so constrained, that any such actions can only be of limited help.

That leaves immigration. I suggest America should make immigration safer (by more carefully investigating new entrants), but not cut it back. It may even be wise to make a small increase in our current immigration rate. America needs to keep growing, and we can fruitfully use both high- and low-skill immigrants. Pluralism works here, as it does in Canada and Australia.

Can pluralism work in Europe? I don't know, and neither do the Europeans. They hate the idea, but they will depopulate if they don't embrace pluralism, via immigration. Perhaps our example can help Europeans see that pluralism might work in the admittedly more complex European context. Japan is probably a hopeless case; perhaps the Japanese should just change the name of their country to Dwindle.

Our non-pluralist Western allies will likely diminish in population, relative power, and influence during [the twenty-first] century. They will become much grayer. Nevertheless, by 2050 there will still be 750 million of them left, so the U.S. needs to keep the Western alliance strong. For all our bickering, let us not forget that the European story in the second half of the twentieth century was a wonderful one: Western Europeans stopped killing each other. Now they are joining hands politically. The next big prize may be Russia. If the Russians choose our path, we will see what [nineteenth-century French political theorist Alexis de] Tocqueville saw: that America and Russia are natural allies.

We must enlist other allies as well. America and India, for instance, are logical partners—pluralist, large, English-speaking, and democratic. We must tell our story. And our immigrants, who come to our land by choice, are our best salesmen. We should extend our radio services to the Islamic world, as we have to the unliberated nations of Asia through Radio Free Asia. The people at the microphones will be U.S. immigrants.

Public Diplomacy

We can lose the contest of civilizations if the developing countries don't evolve toward Western values. One of the best forms of "public diplomacy" is immigration. New immigrants send money home, bypassing corrupt governments—the best kind of foreign aid there is. They go back home to visit and tell their families and friends in the motherland that American modernism, while not perfect, ain't half-bad. Some return home permanently, but they bring with them Western expectations of open government, economic efficiency, and personal liberty. They know that Westernism need not be restricted to the West, and they often have an influence on local politics when they return to their home countries.

Still, because of Europe and Japan, the demographic slide

of Western civilization will continue. And so, America must be prepared to go it alone. If we keep admitting immigrants at our current levels there will be almost 400 million Americans by 2050. That can keep us strong enough to defend and perhaps extend our views and values. And the civilization we will be advancing may not just be Western, but even more universal: American.

"A large flow [of immigrants] can substantially depress the economic opportunities of workers who compete with immigrant labor."

Immigration Strains the Economy

George J. Borjas

Mass immigration puts a strain on the U.S economy, argues George J. Borjas in the following viewpoint. Today's immigrants have fewer skills and are less educated than immigrants in the past and therefore earn lower wages, he points out. Immigrants compete with low-skilled native-born workers for jobs, displacing these workers and driving down the wages for all unskilled laborers. Moreover, Borjas contends, immigrants are more likely to receive public assistance than are natives, and welfare use among the current wave of immigrants is actually increasing. The lower level of economic performance among immigrants persists for several generations, extending the costs of immigration into the future, the author concludes. Borjas is the Pforzheimer Professor of Public Policy at Harvard University's John F. Kennedy School of Government.

As you read, consider the following questions:
1. According to Borjas, how many legal immigrants enter the United States each year?
2. In what way has immigration affected the national high school dropout rate, according to the author?
3. What changes should be made to U.S. immigration policy, in Borjas's opinion?

P articipants in the debate over immigration policy typically use an array of statistics, many of them drawn from the latest research by economists, as weapons in this debate. It is instructive to list the [main] symptoms (not necessarily in order of importance) that frame the immigration debate, and that will likely determine its direction.

1. *The number of immigrants entering the United States is at record levels.*

Although the United States has admitted immigrants throughout its entire history, the number of immigrants admitted into the country has fluctuated greatly over time. Eras of large migration, for instance, were followed by decades of rest, during which time the immigrant waves were presumably assimilated and incorporated into the American mainstream.

Surprisingly, relatively few immigrants (only about 10 million) entered the country between 1820 and 1880. The huge flow that has come to be known as the Great Migration began around 1880 and continued until 1924, bringing with it about 26 million immigrants. The immigration restrictions imposed in 1924, as well as the Great Depression, reduced the immigrant flow to a trickle by the 1930s. Since then, the number of immigrants has increased steadily, with the increase accelerating in the 1970s and 1980s. By the late 1990s, nearly one million persons entered the country legally each year and another 300,000 entered the country illegally.

Because of the increasing number of immigrants and the lower fertility rate of American women, immigration in the 1990s accounted for at least a third of population growth. And this large demographic impact clearly justifies calling the large immigrant wave that began to enter the United States after 1965 the *Second* Great Migration.

Skills and Background

2. *The relative skills and economic performance of immigrants have declined.*

In 1960, the average immigrant man living in the United States actually earned about 4 percent more than the average native man. By 1998, the average immigrant earned about 23 percent less.

The worsening economic performance of immigrants is partly due to a decline in their relative skills across successive waves. The newest immigrants arriving in the country in 1960 were better educated than natives at the time of arrival; by 1998 the newest arrivals had almost two fewer years of schooling. As a result of this growing disadvantage in human capital, the relative wage of successive immigrant waves also fell. At the time of entry, the newest immigrants in 1960 earned 13 percent less than natives; by 1998, the newest immigrants earned 34 percent less.

In short, there has been a precipitous decline—*relative* to the trend in the native population—in the average skills of the immigrant flow reaching the United States. This historic change in the skill composition of the immigrant population helped rekindle the debate over immigration policy, and is the source of many of the symptoms of immigration that are stressed in this debate. . . .

3. *National origin matters.*

Prior to 1965, immigration was guided by the national-origins quota system, which granted visas mainly to persons originating in Western European countries, particularly Great Britain and Germany. The 1965 Amendments to the Immigration and Nationality Act repealed the national origin restrictions, increased the number of available visas, and made family ties to persons already living in the United States the key factor that determines whether a visa applicant is admitted into the country.

As a consequence of these shifts and of major changes in economic and political conditions in the source countries, there was a substantial change in the national origin mix of the immigrant flow. Over two-thirds of the legal immigrants admitted during the 1950s originated in Europe or Canada, one-quarter in Latin America, and only 6 percent in Asia. By the 1990s, only 17 percent of the immigrants originated in Europe or Canada, almost half in Latin America, and 30 percent in Asia.

There are huge differences in economic performance among national origin groups. Immigrants from El Salvador or Mexico earn 40 percent less than natives, while immigrants from Australia or South Africa earn 30 to 40 percent more. These differences in economic performance partly mirror the dispersion in skills across the populations of the source countries. Immigrants who originate in countries that have abundant human capital and higher levels of per-capita income tend to do better in the United States.

The strong link between national origin and economic performance raises an important—and disturbing—problem for immigration policy. Because national origin and immigrant skills are so closely related, any attempt to change one will inevitably change the other.

The Impact on Native Workers

4. *Immigration harms the economic opportunities of the least skilled natives.*

Immigrants cluster geographically in a small number of cities and states. This geographic clustering suggests that one may be able to measure the impact of immigration on the labor market opportunities of native workers by comparing natives who reside in immigrant cities (such as San Diego) with natives who reside in cities where few immigrants live (like Pittsburgh). The available evidence indicates that these "spatial correlations" are extremely weak: if one city has 10 percent more immigrants than another, the native wage in the city with more immigrants is perhaps 0.2 percent lower. This finding has led many observers to conclude that immigration has little impact on native employment opportunities.

However, a weak spatial correlation does not necessarily indicate that immigrants have a numerically inconsequential impact on the well being of native workers. Suppose, for example, that immigration into California lowers the earnings of natives in California substantially. Native workers are not likely to stand idly by and watch their economic opportunities evaporate. Many will move out of California into other regions, and persons who were considering moving to California will now move somewhere else instead. These native population flows effectively diffuse the adverse impact of immigration on California's labor market over the entire economy. In the end, *all* native workers are worse off from immigration, not simply those who happened to live in the areas where immigrants clustered.

There is evidence that the flows of native workers within the United States—as well as the flows of native firms looking for cheap labor—have indeed responded to immigration. Because of these responses, the labor market impact of immigration must be measured at the *national* level, rather than at the local level.

Between 1980 and 1995, immigration increased the number of high school dropouts by 21 percent and the number of persons with at least a high school diploma by only 4 percent. During that time, the wage of high school dropouts relative to that of workers with more schooling fell by 11 percentage points. The disproportionate increase in the number of workers at the bottom end of the skill distribution probably caused a substantial decline in the relative wage of high school dropouts, accounting for perhaps half of the observed drop.

The Economic Impact

5. *Immigration has a severe fiscal impact on the affected states.*

In 1970, immigrants were slightly less likely to receive public assistance than natives. By 1998, immigrants had a much higher chance of receiving welfare: Almost a quarter of immigrant households were receiving *some* type of assistance, as compared to 15 percent of native households.

Two distinct factors account for the disproportionate increase in welfare use among immigrant households. Because more recent immigrant waves are relatively less skilled than earlier waves, it is not surprising that more recent immigrant waves are also more likely to use welfare than earlier waves. In addition, the welfare use of a specific immigrant wave *increases* over time (both in absolute numbers and relative to natives). It seems that the assimilation process involves not only learning about labor market opportunities, but also learning about the income opportunities provided by the welfare state. . . .

6. *The net economic gains from immigration are small.*

Immigrants increase the number of workers in the economy. Because of the additional competition in the labor market, the wage of native workers falls. At the same time, however, native-owned firms gain because they can now hire workers at lower wages; and many native consumers gain because the lower labor costs lead to cheaper goods and services. As with foreign trade, the gains accruing to the persons who use or consume immigrant services exceed the losses suffered by native workers, and hence society as a whole is better off. However, all of the available estimates suggest that the annual net gain is astoundingly small, less than .1 percent of the Gross Domestic Product (GDP). In the late 1990s, this amounted to a net gain of less than $10 billion a year for the entire native population, or less than $30 per person.

There was an old woman who lived in a shoe..

Give me an aspirin

Illegal immigrants

Fischer. © 1994 by *Rochester Post-Bulletin*. Reprinted with permission.

Immigration, however, does more than just increase the total income accruing to natives. Immigration also induces a substantial redistribution of wealth, away from workers who compete with immigrants and toward employers and other users of immigrant services. Workers lose because immigrants drag wages down. Employers gain because immigrants drag wages down. These wealth transfers may be in the tens of billions of dollars per year.

These facts suggest a new prism for interpreting the immigration debate. Immigration is an income redistribution program, a large wealth transfer from those who compete with immigrant workers to those who use immigrant services or buy the goods produced by immigrant workers. The debate over immigration policy, therefore, is not a debate over whether immigration increases the size of the economic pie in the United States. Rather, it is a debate over how the pie is split.

7. *Ethnic skill differentials may persist for at least three generations.*

In 1998, 11 percent of the U.S. population was "second-generation"—born in the United States but with at least one foreign-born parent. By the year 2050, the share of second-generation persons will increase to 14 percent, and an additional 9 percent will be composed of the grandchildren of current immigrants. The economic impact of immigration obviously depends not only on how immigrants adapt, but also on the adjustment process experienced by their offspring.

The historical experience of the children and grandchildren of the First Great Migration provides important lessons about the long-run consequences of immigration. A 20 percent wage differential between two immigrant groups in 1910 implied a 12 percent wage differential in the second generation, and a 5 percent wage differential in the third. In rough terms, about half of the average skill differential between any two groups in the first generation persists into the second, and half of the differential remaining in the second generation persists into the third.

The historical lesson is clear: Skill differentials found among today's immigrants become the skill differentials found among tomorrow's ethnic groups. If past history is any guide, national origin will still determine the economic performance of the grandchildren of the Second Great Migration at the end of the 21st century. In short, ethnicity matters in economic life, and it matters for a very long time. . . .

Implications for Immigration Policy

So what should the United States do?. . .

In the end, a debate over the policy implications of what is known about the economic impact of immigration cannot be based on the evidence alone. *Any policy discussion requires explicitly stated assumptions about what constitutes the national interest.*

Of course, defining the national interest when it comes to immigration policy is very difficult (and very contentious), even when the debate is restricted purely to the economic issues that tend to frame the immigration debate. To see why, divide the world into three distinct constituencies: the current population of the United States ("natives"), the immigrants themselves, and those who remain in the source countries. To draw policy conclusions from the symptoms of immigration, one has to know whose economic welfare the United States should try to improve when setting policy—that of natives, immigrants, the rest of the world, or some mix thereof. The policy implications implied by the symptoms depend crucially on whose interests the United States cares most about. . . .

Suppose that the goal of immigration policy were to maximize the economic well being of the native population. And suppose that native economic well being depends both on per-capita income and on the distribution of income in the native population. In effect, the United States wants immigration to make the country wealthier, but it does not want immigration to greatly increase the amount of inequality in the society.

How many and which types of immigrants should the country then admit? The evidence . . . , I conclude, can be used to make a strong case that the United States would be better off by adopting an immigration policy that favored skilled workers. And a plausible argument can also be made that the country would be better off with a slight reduction in the number of immigrants. . . .

I suspect that an annual flow of 1 million immigrants is probably too large—regardless of whether the losers are at the bottom or at the top of the skill distribution. Such a large flow can substantially depress the economic opportunities of workers who compete with immigrant labor. A good place to start the process of converging to the "magic number" might be to let in 500,000 immigrants per year—which happens to roughly correspond with the recommendation made by the Commission for Immigration Reform in 1997.

> *"Businesses and communities are finding that immigrants, rather than a source of weakness, are helping to stave off the chill of economic hard times."*

Immigration Benefits the Economy

Joel Kotkin

Immigration is good for the economy, argues Joel Kotkin in the following viewpoint. The higher-than-average birth rates among immigrants, as well as an entrepreneurial spirit among the most recent newcomers, is helping to counteract America's current economic recession, Kotkin claims. Immigrants provide a growing consumer market for the technical, energy, and financial services industries, and foreign-born entrepreneurs are starting up small manufacturing, retail, and service businesses, he contends. Kotkin is a senior fellow at the Davenport Institute for Public Policy at Pepperdine University in Malibu, California, and at the Milken Institute in Santa Monica, California.

As you read, consider the following questions:
1. According to Kotkin, why have the assets of Houston's Royal Oaks Bank increased since 2001?
2. What percentage of the businesses in Nick Patel's suburban property developments are occupied by immigrants, according to the author?
3. According to Fred Fu, quoted by the author, what drives the economy?

In January 2001, when Dean Bass and his investors were first putting together $7 million to launch their Royal Oaks Bank, they felt they could ride on a booming Houston economy. With former oilmen in the White House, energy prices high and firms like Enron Corp. on a hiring binge, they looked forward to entering a strong market with powerful demand for business loans.

Much has changed from 2001 to 2002, most notably the fall of energy prices, along with the collapse of one-time civic linchpin Enron, but things are still going well for the upstart bank, whose assets have mushroomed to $33 million in its first year of operation. One of the key reasons, Mr. Bass suggests, has been the continuing growth of Houston's immigrant business community, which now accounts for roughly one in four of the bank's customers.

"The immigrant economy has been a lot less impacted by the energy downturn," suggests Mr. Bass, who has nearly three decades of experience in banking, both as a regulator and executive. "When you look at our customers and our growth, much of it comes from immigrants."

Stave Off the Chill

Royal Oaks' experience is not unique in Houston nor across the country. At a time when the [terrorist attacks] of Sept. 11, 2001, and a recession have resuscitated nativist sentiments, many businesses and communities are finding that immigrants, rather than a source of weakness, are helping to stave off the chill of economic hard times.

Much of this can be traced to their role in stimulating local demand. When international and mainstream domestic demand is slack, many businesses—from banks and real estate firms to retailers—find an internally driven growth market built by a steady stream of energetic newcomers as well as higher than average birth rates.

With their numbers expanding at a rate far faster than native-born Americans, immigrant-dominated groups like Latinos and Asians provide a consumer market that, according to a University of Georgia study, expanded nearly twice as fast in the 1990s as the general population. Today they provide otherwise hard-hit areas with a welcome countercyclical force to counteract the impacts that have devastated local industries, whether high-tech in California, energy in Texas or financial services in New York.

Nor is this merely an inner-city phenomenon, or restricted to traditional immigrant businesses. In Houston, for example, immigrant-led growth has expanded well beyond the inner city to areas such as the Westheimer Corridor in the outer loop where Royal Oaks is situated. In this and surrounding areas, the economy has become increasingly driven by entrepreneurs such as Niranjan "Nick" Patel, who has been developing wide-ranging properties predominately for immigrant operators of fast-food restaurants, convenience stores, motels and gas stations.

These prosaically American businesses out in the vastness of the Houston suburbs are operated by a wide range of entrepreneurs from such diverse countries as India, Pakistan, Vietnam, and Nigeria. Mr. Patel, a leading Royal Oaks borrower, buys and develops the properties for these newcomers, many of whom have arrived in Houston over the past 10 years. Immigrants, the Indian-born Mr. Patel suggests, occupy roughly 60% of the businesses in his over 30 suburban properties.

"People come here to get an education and then hope to start a little business, and then make it grow more," the 49-year-old Mr. Patel says. "They want to settle down in suburbia and become Americans."

An Immigrant-Led Boom

This immigrant-led boom is something that Houston did not have going for it when energy prices crashed in the early 1980s, and devastated much of the local economy. But this is not the same Houston. Over the past decade the city has experienced one of the fastest increases in foreign-born residents—nearly 84% to over 533,000—of any major American city.

In this sense, notes Bill Gilmer, an economist for the Federal Reserve in Houston, immigrants have pushed a greater diversification in the current downturn, opening up various small manufacturing, trade and service businesses. Although these businesses, he suggest, are not immune to the energy and technology slowdowns, he maintains, they feel it less than more traditional mainstream firms.

Nowhere is the evidence of immigrants' abilities to help regions overcome recessions greater than in Southern California, which suffered grievously from the last national downturn a little over a decade ago. Back then, as Anglo homeowners and entrepreneurs were going out of business or escaping to the homogeneous Valhallas of the Intermountain West, Latino, Asian and Middle Eastern newcomers continued to buy and develop properties and industries throughout the region.

An Economic Edge

Immigration gives the United States an economic edge in the world economy. Immigrants bring innovative ideas and entrepreneurial spirit to the U.S. economy. They provide business contacts to other markets, enhancing America's ability to trade and invest profitably in the global economy. They keep our economy flexible, allowing U.S. producers to keep prices down and to respond to changing consumer demands. An authoritative 1997 study by the National Academy of Sciences (NAS) concluded that immigration delivered a "significant positive gain" to the U.S. economy. In testimony before Congress in 2001, Federal Reserve Board Chairman Alan Greenspan said, "I've always argued that this country has benefited immensely from the fact that we draw people from all over the world."

Daniel T. Griswold, *Insight*, March 11, 2002.

As a result, the first property markets to recover in Southern California during the mid-1990s were immigrant-led areas, such as the suburban San Gabriel Valley, east Los Angeles and even South-Central, where many of the new homeowners were Latino. Today much of the eastern and southern reaches of the Los Angeles basin are dotted with shopping centers, factories and other businesses operated by, and often owned by, foreign-born entrepreneurs.

These newcomers, like their counterparts in Houston today, gradually became bulwarks of the resurgent Southern California community. Both the recent President of the Los Angeles Chamber of Commerce, toy distributor Charles Woo, and the chairman of the recent fund-raising campaign for the United Way, banker Dominic Ng, are Hong Kong–

born entrepreneurs who first rose to prominence in the aftermath of the early 1990s' Southern California meltdown.

"When recessions hit, the immigrant population continues to grow and their deposits also increase," suggests Mr. Ng, president of East West Bank, which is based in the heavily Asian San Gabriel Valley east of Los Angeles. "This happened before and it's happening now. Our branches in immigrant areas are doing more business than the others."

Queens Thrives

Today much the same process can even be seen within a few miles of Ground Zero. As Manhattan struggles with the aftermath of Sept. 11, and vacancies there rise, immigrant neighborhoods like Flushing in Queens, where an estimated 70,000 largely Asian immigrants have migrated since the early 1980s, continue to see increases in both occupancies and rents. Although all New York has suffered in the current downturn, Queens' immigrant-dominated economic pockets—such as Flushing, Jackson Heights, Corona and Richmond Hill— stand as relative bastions of economic dynamism.

"Flushing is a different story than Manhattan," reports Fred Fu, the Taiwan-born president of the 300-member Flushing Chinese Business Association. "Everything is occupied and trying to get space is almost impossible. People are still coming to Main Street. People who came here as employees, now want to be owners of homes and businesses. It drives the economy when everyone wants to be an owner."

As Mr. Fu suggests, and experience in Houston and elsewhere demonstrate, the nation's immigrant communities should be seen as a unique asset in battling the current recession and the after-effects of Sept. 11. In helping to sustain even the hardest hit communities, the newest Americans may prove among the most effective Americans of all.

"A large Middle Eastern immigrant population makes it easier for Islamic extremists to operate within the U.S."

Middle Eastern Immigration Threatens National Security

Steven A. Camarota

Many Middle Eastern immigrants are highly educated U.S. citizens who wish to assimilate and adopt American values, Steven A. Camarota explains in the following viewpoint. Currently, however, the majority of Middle Eastern immigrants in the United States are Muslims. Some Muslims resist cultural adaptation by refusing to identify with secular American culture—which could result in political and religious conflicts, Camarota maintains. Moreover, Islamic extremists could readily blend in with a large population of Middle Eastern immigrants, making it easier for them to engage in terrorism on American soil. The author concludes that the overall immigration level should be reduced to protect national security. Camarota is director of research at the Center for Immigration Studies in Washington, D.C.

As you read, consider the following questions:

1. About how many Middle Eastern immigrants are in the United States illegally, according to Camarota?
2. According to the author, what percentage of Middle Eastern immigrants were on welfare in the year 2000?
3. Why is it unlikely that Congress will decide to deny green cards to Middle Easterners, in Camarota's view?

When most people think of immigrants today, they think chiefly of those from Latin America or East Asia. But while most immigrants still come from those regions, an increasing number are coming from a less traditional source: the Middle East. The number of Middle Eastern immigrants in the U.S. has grown nearly eightfold from 1970 to 2000, and is expected to double again by 2010. This growth could have significant repercussions for our homeland security—and our support for Israel.

The Center for Immigration Studies has just issued a study of this group of immigrants, based on new Census Bureau data. (We defined the Middle East broadly, as running roughly from Morocco to Pakistan.) While the overall size of the foreign-born population has tripled since 1970 and now stands at 31 million, the number of immigrants from the Middle East has grown more than twice as fast—from fewer than 200,000 in 1970 to nearly 1.5 million in 2000. Of this population roughly 10 percent, or about 150,000, are illegal aliens (based on Immigration and Naturalization Service estimates).

An Increase in Muslim Immigrants

The new Middle Eastern immigration is not just more numerous than the old, but also very different in religion. While the Mideast itself is overwhelmingly Muslim, historically this has not been true of the region's immigrants to the U.S. Up until the 1960s, Middle Eastern immigrants were mostly Christian Arabs from Lebanon, or Armenians, Assyrians, Greeks, and other Christian minorities fleeing predominantly Muslim countries. In 1970, roughly 15 percent of Middle Eastern immigrants were Muslim: by 2000, almost 73 percent were.

Muslim immigrants and their progeny now number some 2 million. Add in today's perhaps 1 million American converts to Islam—mostly blacks—and you have a total Muslim population of about 3 million. The estimates put out by Muslim advocacy groups of 6 or even 12 million Muslims are almost certainly too high, but it is important to note that—absent a change in U.S. immigration policy—they almost certainly will become true.

We know that interest in emigrating to the U.S. remains

very strong in the Middle East. Even after the September 11, 2001, terror attacks, the State Department in October 2001 received some 1.5 million entries from the region for the visa lottery, which awards 50,000 green cards worldwide to those who win a random drawing. Assuming no change in immigration policy, we project that in just the next decade 1.1 million new immigrants (legal and illegal) from the Middle East will settle in the U.S. Looking forward a little further, within less than 20 years the number of Muslim immigrants and their progeny will grow to perhaps 6 million.

What does this immigration mean for the U.S.? To begin with, immigrants from the Middle East are one of the most highly educated groups in America, with almost half having a bachelor's degree, compared with 28 percent of natives: these education levels should make it easier for them to assimilate. Their average income is higher than that of natives. Another positive sign is their high rates of citizenship: Half are U.S. citizens, compared with 38 percent of immigrants overall. One would think that radicalism would have relatively little appeal for this group, but there are troubling indicators as well. In 2000, nearly one in five Middle Eastern immigrants lived in poverty, compared with about one in ten natives, and 23 percent used at least one major welfare program, compared with only 15 percent of natives. Immigration from the Middle East is no longer an entirely elite phenomenon.

Opinion polls indicate that Middle Eastern immigrants are highly dissatisfied with U.S. policy toward the Arab-Israeli conflict and wish to see a tilt away from support for Israel. Given this, continued Mideast immigration appears likely to lead to changes in U.S. policy, as elected officials respond to Muslim Americans' growing electoral importance. Their increasing political influence was evident earlier in 2002 when three Democratic House members from Michigan, whose districts contain fast-growing Arab immigrant communities, were among only 21 members voting against a resolution expressing solidarity with Israel against terrorism.

Reasons for Concern

On the domestic level, there are three general areas of concern about this influx into the U.S. First, large-scale Mideast immigration is a cause of overworked American consulates overseas. The State Department, by its own admission, is completely overwhelmed by the numbers. In such an environment, it is much more likely that the wrong person will get a visa. Less immigration, of course, would mean that each applicant could be more carefully scrutinized.

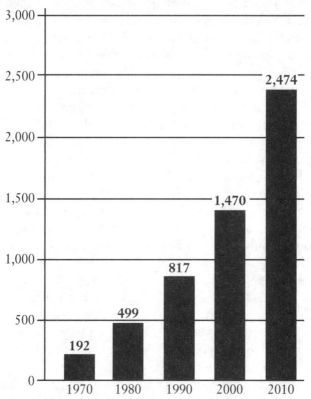

Mideast Immigrants in the United States 1970–2010, in Thousands

Center for Immigration Studies, 2002.

Second, a large Middle Eastern immigrant population makes it easier for Islamic extremists to operate within the U.S. The September 11 hijackers used Middle Eastern immigrant communities for cover. The *Washington Post* has reported that two 9/11 hijackers who lived in San Diego got help from "mosques and established members of [the city's] Islamic community" to "find housing, open a bank account, obtain car insurance—even, at one point, get a job." The *New York Times* has observed that one of the many reasons Islamic terrorists prefer Germany as a base is that it's easier to "blend into a society with a large Muslim population."

Third, and perhaps most important, cultural adaptation poses a special problem for Middle Eastern Muslim immigrants. There has been and continues to be a debate within Islam about whether someone can be a good Muslim while living in the land of unbelievers. There is also a debate among Muslims about whether a good Muslim can give his political allegiance to a secular government, such as ours. that is composed of non-Muslims. Many Muslims can and do become loyal Americans: they have served with distinction in the U.S. military. But for some share of Muslims, coming to identify fully with America will be difficult.

And this problem could become more pronounced over time. To date, the way Middle Eastern immigrants have navigated life in the U.S. reflects the group's relatively small size. A modestly sized group has to accommodate itself to American society, because there is not the critical mass necessary in most cities to support institutions that preserve group customs and identity—such as ethnic-based media outlets, schools, or political and social organizations. But this dynamic is changing as the group grows very rapidly as a result of immigration.

Policy Suggestions

The settlement of 1 million new Mideast immigrants by 2010 will overwhelmingly be the result of legal immigration—but levels of legal immigration can be changed by statute. For example, recently proposed legislation to eliminate the visa lottery would reduce Middle Eastern immigration, because many Mideast immigrants have been using this process to obtain their green cards. Alternatively, an amnesty for illegal aliens would increase Mideast immigration, by creating more legal immigrants who could then sponsor their relatives.

Some conservatives have suggested doing away altogether with immigration from the region, at least until the war on terrorism is over. But such proposals are not really worth debating: Even after September 11, not a single member of Congress proposed cutting off Middle Eastern immigration. Congress would never single out one region of the world for exclusion from green cards. Consider Iraq: Although the U.S. was engaged in open hostilities with that country throughout the 1990s, census data show that 68,000 Iraqi immigrants were allowed into the U.S. during that decade. Moreover, all the countries on the State Department's list of sponsors of terrorism are eligible to send immigrants to the U.S. and have in fact sent hundreds of thousands of legal immigrants here over the last ten years. Congress has never questioned the wisdom of permitting this immigration.

We could, of course, scrutinize visa applicants from some countries with greater care than we take in examining those from, say, Switzerland; it is even possible that Congress would curtail temporary visas in the wake of another attack. But it is politically inconceivable, in our equality-obsessed society, that we would ever return to the days prior to 1965 in which some regions of the world were allotted fewer green cards than others.

Reducing legal immigration from the Mideast is a sensible policy, but the only way this could ever happen would be the enactment of an immigration cap that would apply across the board—to all immigrants, wherever they might hail from. The same holds for efforts to deal with illegal immigration: Given limited resources, in a time of war, it makes sense—over the short term—to pursue with special vigor those immigration-law violators who are Middle Easterners. But over the long term, such a policy would be unfair and politically unsustainable. Reducing the overall immigration level is the wisest plan, for the decades to come.

*"[After the September 11 terrorist attacks],
thousands [of Arabs and Muslims] were
intimidated into not going to work, their
mosques, their schools."*

Middle Eastern and Asian Immigrants Are Unfairly Scapegoated

David Van Biema

In the wake of the September 11, 2001, terrorist attacks, Muslims, Middle Easterners, and South Asian immigrants—and those mistaken for these minorities—are facing discrimination and hate crimes, writes David Van Biema in the following viewpoint. Those perceived as Arab or Muslim have encountered physical attacks, ethnic profiling, and racial harassment. Ironically, however, most U.S. Muslims today were born in America and uphold the same values and loyalties that other citizens do. Moreover, the majority of Arab and South Asian immigrants identify as American and have no sympathy for Islamic terrorists. Van Biema is a writer for *Time* magazine.

As you read, consider the following questions:
1. According to Van Biema, why was Balbir Singh Sodhi shot to death?
2. According to Jamal Badawi, quoted by the author, what are the core concerns of Muslims?
3. Why have Islamist tendencies among Muslim immigrants greatly decreased since the 1980s, according to Van Biema?

David Van Biema, "As American as . . . Although Scapegoated, Muslims, Sikhs and Arabs Are Patriotic, Integrated—and Growing," *Time*, vol. 158, October 1, 2001, p. 72. Copyright © 2001 by Time, Inc. Reproduced by permission.

He wanted a congenial space where people might gather, which is why Balbir Singh Sodhi was outside his Chevron station in Mesa, Arizona [on September 22, 2001], surveying the vinca and sage he had just planted. Says Guru Roop Kaur Khalsa, one of Sodhi's ministers: "Even though it was just a gas station, he saw it as a center of the community. He looked for innocence and sweetness and tried to capture it." Then, police allege, a man named Frank Silva Roque drove by in a black Chevy pickup and pumped three bullets into Sodhi, killing him almost instantly, mocking innocence and sweetness. Sodhi appears to have died because he looked Muslim. He was not. He was a Sikh, and his religion was born as a reform of Hinduism. But to some, the turban and beard that most Sikhs wear look like [terrorist] Osama bin Laden's. When the police caught Roque, they claim he explained his actions by saying. "I'm an American."

Imagine this: you wake up every morning nervous, stalked by faceless enemies. It is nothing personal; they just hate what they think you represent. The attack could come at any time, and there is virtually no defense. If that seems to describe all America at the moment, there is one group for whom the unbearable tension since the World Trade Center attack [on September 11, 2001] is doubled. If you are a Muslim or an Arab, or look like one to someone focused primarily on his own rage, you must fear not only bin Laden-style terrorism but also the insults, blows and bullets of your countrymen.

[On September 27, 2001] someone threw stone after stone through the windshields of cabs in Manhattan's Central Park, apparently targeting dark-skinned drivers. "A lot of cabdrivers are not driving," says Ali Agha Abba, a Pakistani-American taxi driver in New York City. "I can't afford to not work. So I have to take a chance." [On September 24, 2001] a man drove a Mustang through the front entrance of the Grand Mosque in Parma, Ohio, the largest in the state. The Sunday before, a Muslim woman in Memphis was beaten on her way to worship. The day before that, a Pakistani Muslim store owner was shot and killed. The FBI called it a hate crime.

True, George [W.] Bush spoke out for Muslims at a mosque and before Congress [in late September 2001], telling them, "We respect your faith. Its teachings are good and peaceful."

[On September 25] FBI agents began a round of bureau meetings with local Muslim and Arab leaders in various states, asking for their help with investigations and assuring their protection. Said a relieved participant: "We know we have the FBI behind us."

And yet . . . on [September 24] Louisiana Congressman John Cooksey told a radio show, "If I see someone come in that's got a diaper on his head, that guy needs to be pulled over." (He later apologized.) On that same day, the pilot of a Delta flight in Texas had a Pakistani American removed before takeoff because he said his crew did not feel comfortable with the man aboard. Delta offered him a new ticket—on another carrier. (It later apologized.) In Lincoln, Rhode Island, someone hit a pregnant woman wearing a hijab (head scarf) with a stone. She has been calling midwives to avoid giving birth in the hospital because "I don't want to go to any public place." A CNN/*USA Today*/Gallup poll of 1,032 adults indicated that 49% thought all Arabs—American citizens included—should have to carry special ID cards.

All told, the Council on American-Islamic Relations [C.A.I.R.] counts more than 600 "incidents" since Sept. 11 [2001], victimizing people thought to be Arab or Muslim, including four murders, 45 people assaulted and 60 mosques attacked. Thousands were intimidated into not going to work, their mosques, their schools. Some 200 Muslims are estimated to have died in the Twin Towers. Yet, says C.A.I.R.'s Nihad Awad. "Muslims are being accused of something that the community has not done, and it's really an awkward and unfair position to be in." Thousands of answering machines—and actual people—fielded calls like the one that came into the offices of a Muslim organization in Santa Clara, Calif.: "We should bomb your ass and blow you back home." The caller was apparently unaware that "home" is here.

There is no God but Allah, and Muhammad is his prophet. Pray five times a day. Give alms. Fast during the month of Ramadan. If you are capable, make a pilgrimage to Mecca. If these "five pillars" seem foreign to you, you may not be talking with your neighbors. Islam is an American religion. There are some 7 million Muslims in the U.S. That's more than the number of Jews and more than twice the number of

Episcopalians. Thirty years ago, the Islamic count was a mere 500,000. The number of mosques rose from 598 in 1986 to 1,372 in 2001. The number of American-born Muslims now far exceeds the count of immigrants.

Attacks on Muslims

Much to the dismay of American Muslims, verbal attacks on Islam and Muslims by conservative commentators, religious clergy, and elected officials are increasing in our nation at an alarming rate. . . .

Syndicated columnist Ann Coulter made perhaps some of the most vicious comments [after the September 11, 2001, terrorist attacks] writing that America "should invade their [Muslim] countries, kill their leaders and convert them to Christianity." She also called for the "mass deportation" of Muslims. And [columnist] Paul Craig Roberts wrote: "Of all the hyphenated-Americans, Muslims pose the greatest challenge." Roberts also objected to "persons of Middle Eastern origin searching the personal effects of native-born blue-eyed blond mothers," in a thinly-veiled racist reference to Middle Eastern–appearing airport security screeners. Some evangelical clergymen have also joined in the fray. Franklin Graham, son of evangelist Billy Graham, is refusing to retract inflammatory remarks in which he claimed: "The God of Islam is not the same God. . . It's a different God, and I believe it is a very evil and wicked religion." In the NBC report, Graham (who delivered the benediction at President George W. Bush's inauguration) said, "I don't believe this [Islam] is this wonderful, peaceful religion." Concurring with Graham's comments, Reverence Chuck Colson, former Richard Nixon aide and founder of Prison Fellowship Ministries, said: "I agree that Islam is a religion, which, if taken seriously, promotes violence."

Riad Z. Abdel Karim, *Washington Report on Middle East Affairs*, January/February 2002.

Islam, the youngest of the major faiths, was influenced by Judaism and Christianity. Muslims are "people of the book," accepting the Jewish Bible and the New Testament as Holy Scripture while maintaining that the Koran's famously elegant and expressive Arabic is God's final and inerrant word. Similarly, followers of Islam believe Moses, John the Baptist and Jesus were prophets but the final messenger was Muhammad, to whom, they say, the angel Gabriel dictated the Koran. Like Christians and Jews, says Jamal Badawi, a religion professor at Saint Mary's University in Halifax, [Nova Scotia], their core concerns are "moral behavior, love of neighbor, justice and compassion. We believe that we are created for a purpose, and we are going to be held responsible for our life on earth on the day of judgment." Muslims do not worship Muhammad (who, unlike Moses or Jesus, was a lavishly documented historical figure, dying in A.D. 632) but regard him as exemplary. It is upon the Koran and collections of his sayings (Hadiths) that Islamic law, or Sharia, is based. . . .

It is a point of Islamic pride that a Muslim can walk into any mosque anywhere in the world and participate in the service. That said, the Islamic population in the U.S. is almost as varied as Mecca's. The first Muslims here were African slaves, who were forcibly Christianized, although some Muslim descendants still live on the Georgia coast. Syrians and Lebanese began arriving in the late 1800s. But the three largest groups in America are made up of more recent additions.

The largest is African American, a group of almost 2 million whose story is unknown to most of their countrymen. In the 1930s, Wallace D. Fard and his acolyte Elijah Muhammad founded a group called the Nation of Islam. The Nation was misnamed: its racialist views and unique theology cause most Muslims to see it as non-Islamic. Elijah's son Wallace, however, was trained in classical Arabic and, following in the footsteps of his friend Malcolm X, made a Meccan pilgrimage. After Malcolm's murder and Elijah Muhammad's death, Wallace changed his name to Warith Deen Muhammad and gradually led his flock to mainstream Sunni Muslim observance. Although Louis Farrakhan eventually reactivated the Nation name and attracted some 25,000 adherents, W.D. Muhammad is the effective leader of 1.6 million believers. He is regarded by many as a mujaddid, a once-in-a-century "renewer of the faith." . . .

The remaining two large American Islamic blocs have roughly parallel histories. The majority of Arab and South Asian (Indian subcontinental) believers began arriving here in the late 1960s in response to changes in immigration law and home-country programs that subsidized study here. The students became professionals and put down roots. They were joined by relatives and by refugees from various international upheavals. Most, while thrilled at America's free speech and its economic prospects, were shocked by the materialism, secularism and free morality that they encountered. Settling into lives as doctors, engineers or grocery-store owners, they contended with malls, disco and recurrent spasms of anti-Arab and -Muslim sentiment fueled by events such as the Arab oil boycott and the first World Trade Center bombing. Many also had vivid memories of American involvement in their home nations. A sizable faction was attracted to the Islamist movement, which argued for isolation from the American social and political system in favor of an eventual Muslim triumph. "The process of Americanization," wrote Georgetown's [Yvonne] Haddad in 1987, "is impeded."

But 14 years later, Haddad reports, Islamist sympathy is below 10%. What happened? The new immigrants became more comfortable with the language and the culture around them. They realized that unlike many of their homelands, one could express political or cultural opposition here and still be regarded as a good American. And finally, they gave birth to a generation, now in its 20s and 30s. whose primary identification is American, albeit with a "Muslim" prefix. "The feeling is," paraphrases Haddad (who is not Muslim), "'We are American. We participate in this America. We cannot live off America and not be part of it, and we have something to contribute.'". . .

That is not to say there may not be a tiny minority of mosques in America whose congregants tilt toward the Taliban[1] or even bin Laden. At the Hazrat-I-Abubakr Sadiq mosque in Queens, after the imam decried the World Trade attack to his 1,000-person congregation, members of the Taliban's Pashtun clan moved to the basement in apparent protest.

Omar Abdel Rahman, the jailed ringleader of the 1993 World Trade Center bombing, used to preach at the Masjid al-Salaam mosque in Jersey City, New Jersey. The day after the [terrorist attacks], two men arrested on a train in Dallas

---

1. The Taliban was an Islamic fundamentalist sect that ruled Afghanistan from 1996 to 2001.

with box cutters, hair dye and more than $5,000 in cash are reported to have worshiped there recently. Two cops now stand at the mosque door.

Two days before the attack, Moataz al-Hallak, the former imam at the Center Street mosque in Arlington, Texas, returned there to pray. It turns out that al-Hallak was close to Wadih el-Hage, bin Laden's secretary who was recently found guilty in the U.S. embassy bombings in East Africa. Al-Hallak's name also reportedly showed up on a list at a Brooklyn refugee center headed by several men convicted in the 1993 Trade Center bombing. Al-Hallak, who has not been charged in either World Trade plot, has denied connection to bin Laden and claims to have counseled el-Hage only on religious matters. Najam Khan, president of the group that runs the Arlington mosque, says it fired al-Hallak [in 2000] for neglecting his flock—before the bin Laden connections were known. "I don't think he was preaching violence per se," Khan says, looking mournful. "We feel this mosque is being targeted because of individuals who may have had shady business somewhere, but that has nothing to do with the mosque and the rest of the community." He says the imam never talked politics from the pulpit: "It doesn't make sense. No mosque wants that. It divides people."

When Muslim immigrant groups first started arriving in the '60s, says Professor Haddad, "they looked at each other and said, 'I have nothing to do with you.'" Today all that has changed. C.A.I.R.'s Mosque in America project reports that only 7% of the 12,000 mosques surveyed serve a single ethnic group. Almost 90% play host to a mix of African Americans, South Asian Americans and Arab Americans.

Think about that: the Arabic word for all those who affirm Islam is *ummah*. It implies a sense of oneness and community. Around the world and over the centuries, as Islamic empires have collided, it has often been difficult to discern. But here in America, the country where Sunday is the most segregated day of the week, it flourishes. Balbir Singh Sodhi's killer would probably not have appreciated that. But Sodhi would have, despite not being a Muslim. And maybe there is something here for all Americans to learn, if we can only catch our breath.

Periodical Bibliography

The following articles have been selected to supplement the diverse views presented in this chapter.

Robert J. Bresler	"Immigration: The Sleeping Time Bomb," *USA Today* (Magazine), July 2002.
Ronald Brownstein	"Green Light, Red Light: Is the Push to Liberalize Immigration Policy a Casualty of the Surprise Terrorist Attacks on September 11?" *American Prospect*, November 19, 2001.
Joseph A. D'Agostino	"Immigration from Middle East to U.S. Increasing," *Human Events*, September 23, 2002.
Samuel Francis	"The Conquest of the United States by Mexico," *Wanderer*, July 11, 2002.
Dagoberto Gilb	"Ebb and Flow: Colors of Our World," *Los Angeles Times*, July 5, 2001.
Ted Hayes	"Illegal Immigration Threatens U.S. Sovereignty, Economy and Culture," *Insight*, September 25, 2000.
Tamar Jacoby	"Too Many Immigrants?" *Commentary*, April 2002.
Dick Kirschten	"America's Demographic Divide," *National Journal*, January 16, 1999.
Charles Krauthammer	"Immigrants Are America's Future," *San Diego Union-Tribune*, July 19, 1998.
Mary M. Kritz	"Time for a National Discussion on Immigration," *International Migration Review*, Spring 2002.
Lisa Suhair Majaj	"Who Are the Arab Americans?" *Cobblestone*, May 2002.
Gregory Rodriguez	"Forging a New Vision of America's Melting Pot," *New York Times*, February 11, 2001.
Candice Rondeaux and Asjylyn Loder	"Latino Laborers Targeted," *National Catholic Reporter*, September 7, 2001.
Susan Sachs	"Cracking the Door for Immigrants," *New York Times*, July 1, 2001.
AnnaLee Saxenian	"Brain Circulation: How High-Skill Immigration Makes Everyone Better Off," *Brookings Review*, Winter 2002.

CHAPTER 3

How Should the United States Address Illegal Immigration?

Chapter Preface

On March 22, 2000, the frozen body of twenty-year-old Jose Luis Uriostegua was discovered on Mount Laguna in east San Diego County, nearly twenty miles north of the U.S.-Mexico border. Uriostegua had fled from Guerrero, a poverty-stricken state in Mexico, in hopes of finding a better life for himself and his family in the United States. When his remains were found, Uriostegua was identified as "Number 500"—the five hundredth person to die while trying to elude the U.S. Border Patrol under California's "Operation Gatekeeper" program.

Operation Gatekeeper began in 1994 as a U.S. Immigration and Naturalization (INS) strategy to prevent illegal immigrants from crossing the Mexico-California border. The strategy places an increased number of Border Patrol agents, extensive fencing, new roads, stadium-type lights, motion detectors, infrared night scopes, and computerized identification systems along urban border-crossing routes. Migrants who wish to evade capture are thus forced to travel in much more dangerous terrain—either steep mountainous areas with dense vegetation or desert country with no shade or water. Critics denounce the INS for contributing to more than fifteen hundred migrant deaths through its Operation Gatekeeper and similar border-enforcement programs in Arizona, New Mexico, and Texas.

In response to the growing concern over these immigrant deaths, the INS launched "Operation Lifesaver" in June 1998, using patrol flights and search-and-rescue missions to find migrants in distress. But such "after the fact" assistance is hardly of help, contends Claudia Smith of the California Rural Legal Assistance Foundation: "As long as the strategy is to maximize the dangers by moving the migrant foot traffic out of the urban areas and into the mountains and deserts . . . the deaths will keep multiplying." Most ironically, critics maintain, this strategy does not effectively curtail illegal residency. Journalist Susan Luzzaro states, "Because it is too dangerous and too costly to return home, immigrants are obliged to stay . . . ; Gatekeeper has created a permanent buildup of immigrants on the United States side of the border."

Other analysts, however, believe that the criticisms of border-enforcement policies are misdirected. These commentators maintain that the United States has a right to prevent undocumented immigration and contend that the Border Patrol is simply constructing a more secure boundary. Immigrant smugglers—and the illegal immigrants themselves—make their own choices to face the dangers of rugged terrain, they assert. According to columnist Samuel Francis, "The aliens who died were indeed poor people—not just because they died but because they were in fact being exploited by both the hoodlums they paid to guide them as well as by the . . . open-borders nuts who lure them into this country in the first place." In the end, Francis maintains, "The ultimate blame for the deaths of the poor people trying to enter illegally must fall on them. They knew what they were doing was illegal and dangerous—and they did it anyway."

A central question posed in the controversy over illegal immigration is what immigration policies would be most effective and humane. The authors in the following chapter address this question in their discussions of border policy and immigrant amnesty.

"Considerable success has been achieved in restoring integrity and safety to the Southwest border."

U.S Border Patrol Strategies Help Prevent Illegal Immigration

U.S. Border Patrol

In the following viewpoint, the U.S. Border Patrol outlines the strategies it has utilized since the mid-1990s to reduce illegal immigration to the United States. These strategies focus on disrupting traditional routes used by illegal aliens in the Southwest, updating detection technology, improving infrastructure, and increasing manpower to thwart unlawful border crossings. These tactics greatly boost the chance that illegal entrants will be caught and will effectively deter those who are considering unlawful immigration, the authors maintain. The Border Patrol is the mobile, uniformed enforcement arm of the U.S. Department of Homeland Security.

As you read, consider the following questions:
1. What does the Border Patrol mean by the phrase "prevention through deterrence"?
2. By how much have alien smugglers raised their fees since the Border Patrol has utilized its new strategies, according to the authors?
3. According to the Border Patrol, how do border operations improve the life of border communities?

U.S. Border Patrol, "The National Border Patrol Strategy," www.bcis.gov, Bureau of Citizenship and Immigration Services, U.S. Department of Homeland Security, September 9, 2002.

The 1994–1995 immigration initiatives included a Border Patrol Program enhancement to build on the Clinton administration's commitment to reform the immigration system. The Commissioner of the Immigration and Naturalization Service recognized the need to address the immigration challenges of asylum, technology, criminal aliens, naturalization, and control of the border in an efficient, comprehensive and coordinated manner. In that context, the Border Patrol developed a systematic approach to strengthen control of the border, restricting the passage of illegal traffic and encouraging legal entry as the preferred method to enter the United States.

The strategy specifically calls for "prevention through deterrence," that is, elevating the risk of apprehension to a level so high that prospective illegal entrants would consider it futile to attempt to enter the U.S. illegally. Rather than relying on traditional methods that historically worked well, but resulted in a fluctuating level of border control, the strategy concentrates resources in phases to the areas of greatest illegal activity, currently certain targeted entry corridors of the Southwest border. Future concentrations will be in the remainder of the Southwest border, the coastal states, Puerto Rico, and the Northern border.

The Southwest Border Strategy

In February 1994, Attorney General Janet Reno and Immigration and Naturalization Service (INS) Commissioner Doris Meissner announced an innovative, multi-year strategy to strengthen enforcement of the nation's immigration laws and to disrupt the traditional illegal immigration corridors along the nation's Southwest border. Under the bold strategy, new personnel, backed with equipment and infrastructure improvements, are deployed in targeted areas each year, starting with the most vulnerable areas.

This strategy treats the entire border as a single, seamless entity. Enforcement activities between the ports-of-entry are integrated fully with those taking place in the ports, which the strategy recognizes as both vital to the nation's economy and potential entry points for criminals and contraband. As a result, INS has been able to enhance its enforcement capabilities while dramatically reducing waiting times for those trying to cross the border legally. The strategy uses a phased approach beginning in the Southwest until control is achieved nationwide.

Considerable success has been achieved in restoring integrity and safety to the Southwest border by implementing the strategy through well-laid-out multi-year operations, such as Operation Gatekeeper in San Diego, California, Operation Hold the Line in El Paso, Texas, Operation Rio Grande in McAllen, Texas, and Operation Safeguard in Tucson, Arizona. The initial phases of these operations typically result in an increase in apprehensions, reflecting the deployment of more agents and enhanced technology. However, as the deterrent effect takes hold, the number of apprehensions declines as the operation gains control over the area.

Operation Gatekeeper: California

Launched in October 1994, *Operation Gatekeeper* has proven that deterrence works. Initially, the operation focused on five miles of Imperial Beach that accounted for nearly 25 percent of all illegal border crossings nationwide. Once the Border Patrol regained control of this heavily trafficked stretch, Gatekeeper was expanded to include the entire 66 miles of border under the San Diego Sector's jurisdiction. As a result, apprehensions in Fiscal Year (FY) 2001 reached a 28-year low in the sector, which accounted for 45 percent of all apprehensions nationwide before Gatekeeper but only 9 percent in FY 2001.

Spurred by these dramatic results, INS extended Gatekeeper in FY 1998 into California's Imperial Valley. The expanded operation targets alien smuggling rings that moved to the El Centro area in response to the increased Border Patrol presence in San Diego.

Under the El Centro initiative, in FY 1998, 140 agents were detailed to the El Centro Sector, an 80 percent increase in manpower level that gave the Sector the ability to staff checkpoint operations around the clock. Apprehensions climbed to more than 226,580 in FY 1998, an increase of 55 percent over FY 1997.

In FY 1999, 78 agents were deployed to El Centro. In the next few years, as the operation takes hold, apprehensions are expected to decline. A clear indication of the initiative's deterrent effect is that alien smugglers have raised their fees from $250 per person to as much as $1,500.

Texas and New Mexico

Operation Hold the Line, initiated in the El Paso Sector in 1993, produced a 50 percent decline in apprehensions from FY 1993 to FY 1996. Building on that success, INS launched *Operation Rio Grande* in August 1997 to gain control of the border in the Rio Grande Valley and ultimately expand the coverage of these two operations across all of Texas and New Mexico. The plan developed by INS field managers was tailored to meet unique local challenges and conditions. As part of Rio Grande, 260 new Border Patrol Agent positions were added to the McAllen Sector and 205 positions to the Laredo Sector in FY 1998, increases of 34 percent and 46 percent respectively over 1997. The agents' effectiveness was enhanced by the deployment of resource multiplying technology such as infrared scopes, night-vision goggles,

---

Regaining Control of the Border

Throughout the 1980's and early 90's the 14-mile stretch of border in San Diego, California, was hostile, violent, and out of control. Border patrol agents use terms like "chaos" and "anarchy" to describe it, saying that they faced riot conditions every night. Crowds would gather on the Tijuana side and pelt border-patrol agents with rocks. Shots were sometimes fired across the border at patrolling agents, and almost daily thousands of Mexicans would gather on the U.S. side, then dash forward en masse in what were known as banzai runs. . . .

It was in El Paso, Texas, however, that the first attempt to regain control of the border was undertaken. In 1994 Silvestre Reyes, then chief of the El Paso sector of the border patrol and now a U.S. congressman, devised a plan called Operation Blockade, later renamed Hold the Line. It focused not on apprehension once illegals had crossed the border, but rather on deterring them from trying to cross in the first place. Operation Hold the Line combined fences, technology, and close monitoring by agents stationed along the border. The result was a significant drop in illegal entry and other crimes in the El Paso area.

Glynn Custred, *The American Spectator*, October 2000.

---

underground sensors, and IDENT (an automated finger-print identification system) terminals. Infrastructure along the border was also improved by installing fences and constructing all-weather roads.

Operation Rio Grande is divided into three targeted corridors. The operation began, and is now firmly established, in Corridor 1, encompassing McAllen, Brownsville and Laredo.

In FY 1998 apprehensions decreased by 35 percent in the Brownsville area and by 27 percent in Laredo from the last fiscal year. The flow of illegal immigrant traffic shifted to other corridors. Falfurrias Station, in Corridor 2, experienced a nearly 40 percent increase in apprehensions over FY 1997. The 500 agents deployed in FY 1999 expanded the coverage of *Operation Rio Grande* as well as maintained the success of *Operation Hold the Line*, ultimately leading to greater control over illegal entries across Texas and New Mexico.

Rio Grande has provided clear evidence that border operations improve the quality of life in border communities by contributing to falling crime rates. Both Brownsville and Laredo reported a drop in criminal activity during FY 1998, with the crime rate falling by more than 20 percent in Brownsville alone. These results mirror the decline in criminal activities that has accompanied INS operations in other areas, including San Diego and El Paso.

Operation Safeguard: Arizona

Launched in FY 1995, *Operation Safeguard* redirected illegal border crossings away from urban areas near the Nogales port-of-entry to comparatively open areas that the Border Patrol could more effectively control. By moving potential crossers away from urban areas where they were able to disappear into local communities, the Border Patrol has taken advantage of new equipment and technology and increased staffing to make apprehensions in areas where illegal entrants are more visible. Today there are more than 1,000 agents on duty in the sector compared to fewer than 300 prior to FY 1994.

As in other operations, the infusion of agents has been backed by a wealth of new equipment and technology. In addition to IDENT terminals, crucial improvements include the installation of 19 additional remote low-light surveillance cameras along the border in Nogales and Douglas making it possible for one officer to monitor border activity at several different locations simultaneously, freeing up more agents to patrol the line.

In January, 1999, 145 agents were detailed to the Nogales area. As part of the FY 1999 expansion of *Operation Safeguard*, Tucson Sector received 350 new Border Patrol Agent positions. In addition to increased manpower, border access roads in the greater Nogales area were improved. In addition, four miles of border lighting in Nogales and three miles of lighting in Douglas were installed, expanding the existing 1.3 miles already in place.

Northern Border Initiatives

Illegal immigration across the Northern border has been through attempts at ports-of-entry using traditional means, such as false claims to U.S. citizenship, misrepresented purpose for entry, and fraudulent or improper documentation, and through entry without inspection between ports. A plan to address the areas outside the Southwest border is in the final stages of completion and has not been officially approved by INS.

*"More than 1,450 migrant workers have
died along the border since 1995 as a
result of Operation Gatekeeper and its
counterparts in Arizona and Texas."*

U.S. Border Patrol Strategies Are Cruel and Ineffective

Justin Akers

Current U.S. Border Patrol strategies create deadly and torturous situations for migrant workers, Justin Akers argues in the following viewpoint. Operation Gatekeeper and similar approaches to reducing illegal immigration place extra police and Border Patrol agents along commonly traveled migrant corridors; in addition, new fences, canals, sensors, and lights have been installed at traditional crossing routes. To avoid being caught, undocumented migrants have started crossing the border in rugged desert and mountain regions where they risk death from exposure to extreme heat or cold. Moreover, Akers reports, illegal immigrants have encountered human rights abuses—including beatings, sexual abuse, and medical neglect—while being detained by the Border Patrol. Akers is a member of the International Socialist Organization in San Diego, California.

As you read, consider the following questions:
1. According to Akers, what kinds of military hardware have been integrated into border operations?
2. In the author's opinion, how effective is Operation Gatekeeper in reducing illegal immigration?
3. What is the relationship between capitalism and anti-immigration policies, in Akers' view?

Justin Akers, "Operation Gatekeeper: Militarizing the Border," *International Socialist Review*, June/July 2001, pp. 68–72. Copyright © 2001 by *International Socialist Review*. Reproduced by permission.

In the early evening hours of June 12, 1992, 26-year-old Dario Miranda Valenzuela planned to cross the border into the United States through Southern Arizona. Like many others heading north at various points along the U.S.–Mexico border, Dario was to look for work that evening to take some money back to his family in the border town of Nogales, Mexico. As Dario began to cross the rugged canyon, gunshots rang out in the distance. As he fled from the direction of the shots, two bullets from a high-powered AR-15 rifle struck him in the back. Border Patrol agent Michael Elmer, a veteran of the force, had shot the unarmed Dario as a suspected "drug scout," even though there was no proof of this other than the fact that Dario was running. As Dario bled to death, Agent Elmer dragged him 50 yards away to hide him until Elmer could return later to "bury the evidence." Dario soon died from his wounds. While the incident was uncovered and Elmer was brought to trial for his actions, the jury found him not guilty of all charges. They stated that he acted in self-defense in a tense border area "war zone."

Alejandro Kassorla, a 23-year-old cane cutter, decided to try to cross the border into the U.S. because he was having trouble supporting his family in Mexico. When he traveled to the U.S. six years before, he had come home with enough money to build a small home for his wife and two children. He got together with his friend Samuel and a married couple, Javier and Elvia, who also wanted to cross. The smugglers they paid to guide them said it would be a short trip through the rugged mountains near San Diego, but in fact the trip usually took three days. After temperatures dropped below freezing on the third day, the smugglers abandoned Alejandro and his group. When Javier and Samuel began to suffer from hypothermia, Alejandro and Elvia went for help. After Alejandro collapsed from hypothermia, Elvia went on. When she finally returned with help, the other three had already frozen to death.

These two stories capture the impact of "Operation Gatekeeper," a U.S. government strategy to seal off popular border-crossing points using a combination of new border fences, an increase in border personnel, and the latest military hardware and training. Border policing is carried out with the participation of various military agencies. Operation Gatekeeper has forced migrants from Mexico to cross the border in more remote mountainous areas, where they are subject to extreme heat and cold. While the Immigration and Naturalization Service (INS) promotes this program as a policy of "prevention through deterrence," Gatekeeper is, in reality, a death sentence for many immigrants crossing the border and the latest policy directed at controlling the flow of Mexican labor.

Operation Gatekeeper's Deadly Toll

"We must not tolerate illegal immigration," wrote then-President Bill Clinton in 1996. He boasted, "Since 1992, we have increased our Border Patrol by over 35 percent; deployed underground sensors, infrared night scopes, and encrypted radios; built miles of new fences; and installed massive amounts of new lighting." Operation Gatekeeper was launched in 1994 by the Clinton administration as part of Clinton's get-tough policy on illegal immigration. Similar operations were also launched or already existed in other regions along the U.S.–Mexico border. The operation aimed to stop the flow of immigrants by concentrating military and police forces along traditional crossing routes on the border to seal them off. To fund this buildup, the budget for the INS nearly tripled to $4.6 billion annually.

Originally spanning 66 miles from the Pacific Ocean through San Diego, California, and into the mountains, Operation Gatekeeper has been expanded into Yuma, Arizona. It includes a 73-mile 10-foot-high steel wall. Secondary fences span 52 of those miles, and a triple fence spans the stretch from the Pacific Ocean to the Otay Mountains. Similar operations exist along stretches in Arizona and Texas. More military hardware, such as Black Hawk helicopters, heat sensors, night-vision telescopes, electronic vision detection devices, and computerized fingerprinting equipment, has also been integrated into border operations. Gatekeeper has also seen a dramatic increase in agents, with nearly 8,500 currently working in the border region.

The result has not been to curb or reduce immigration, but to create a more deadly situation for migrant workers. A deadly militarized border force at the traditional crossing points has forced the majority of workers to cross through rugged terrain. It has pushed them east, through the Otay Mountains and the desert beyond them. In the Otay Mountains, peaks reach as high as 6,000 feet, with freezing temperatures six months out of the year. In the desert beyond the mountains, temperatures climb as high as 120 degrees with sand dunes that reach 300 feet. It is in this situation that the most egregious effects of Gatekeeper take their toll.

According to Doris Meissner, former chief of the INS, "We did believe geography would be an ally." She was correct. The policy has resulted in the deaths of more than 600 immigrants in the San Diego–Yuma stretch alone since its inception in 1994. According to a human rights investigation conducted by the American Civil Liberties Union, most of the deaths can be attributed to exposure to freezing temperatures in the mountains during the winter and to the heat of the desert in the Imperial Valley in the summer.

A Cynical Disregard for Life

The deaths don't just occur along the California–Mexico border. In May 2000, 14 migrants were found dead after attempting to cross miles of desert in 115-degree heat at a place Border Patrol agents call "The Devil's Path" near Yuma, Arizona. "Nobody should be surprised by these deaths," said Claudia Smith, a lawyer for the California Rural Legal Assistance Foundation. "They are an entirely foreseeable consequence of moving the migrant traffic out of the urban areas and into the most remote and dangerous areas."

Another significant portion of the deaths can be attributed to drowning, as migrants attempt to escape the heat by crossing through the All-American Canal and other border canals and rivers. The New River, one such crossing point, is one of the most polluted rivers in the border region. It is favored because the Border Patrol agents won't go near it.

The cynical use of this policy becomes clear when it is revealed that the actual blueprint assumes that "most of the 'influx' would not be deterred by the 'mortal dangers' which came with the new routes." As one INS supervisor explained in the *San Diego Union-Tribune* in 1996, "Eventually, we'd like to see them all out in the desert." This complete disregard for the lives of migrant workers is why hundreds are allowed to die crossing the border in California. Staggeringly, more than 1,450 migrant workers have died along the border since 1995 as a result of Operation Gatekeeper and its counterparts in Arizona and Texas. All told, since the launch of Operation Gatekeeper in 1994, the number of deaths has increased by 500 percent.

All of this is fine for Washington. According to Meisner, it would take five more years of operations such as Gatekeeper to assert a "reasonable level of control" along the entire border. If immigration levels stay constant, Meisner can expect at least 2,000 more deaths over this period in California alone.

Human Rights Abuses

While the death toll rises from Operation Gatekeeper, other forms of terror and abuse can be attributed to the Border Patrol and other U.S. agencies. According to a report by Amnesty International that condemns Operation Gatekeeper:

> The allegations of ill-treatment Amnesty International collected include people struck with batons, fists and feet, often as punishment for attempting to run away from Border Patrol agents; denial of food, water and blankets for many hours while detained in Border Patrol stations and at Ports of Entry for INS processing; sexual abuse of men and women; denial of medical attention, and abusive, racially derogatory and unprofessional conduct towards the public sometimes resulting in the wrongful deportation of US citizens to Mexico. People who reported that they had been ill-treated included men, women and children, almost exclusively of Latin American descent. They included citizens and legal permanent residents of the USA, and members of Native American First Nations whose tribal lands span the U.S.–Mexico border.

The brutality and disregard displayed by the Border Patrol has enabled and encouraged racist and vigilante acts against migrants as well.

Ranchers in Arizona and Texas have gone so far as to "hunt" for immigrants. One South Texas landowner was offended when a migrant asked him for water after walking through the brush for days to avoid the Border Patrol. According to subsequent charges, the landowner fired on the man and calmly watched him die. Elsewhere in Texas, numerous other shootings by ranchers have occurred.

In another situation, a rancher from Arizona would hunt for migrants with his brother and their M-16 rifles as punishment for drinking their water and leaving trash on their land. When asked about this, and the fact that the brothers were inviting tourists to join in the hunts, a Border Patrol officer remarked to the press that they "appreciated the help." Along with violent ranchers, other vigilante groups have set up patrols along the border, including right-wing "citizen" groups, the Ku Klux Klan, and the skinhead group White Aryan Resistance.

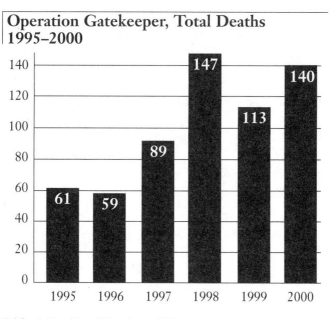

Operation Gatekeeper, Total Deaths 1995–2000

California Rural Legal Foundation, 2001.

Joint operations with military personnel have also proven deadly for all people in the border region. Joint patrols have been conducted regularly with other government and military agencies. Joint Task Force 6 (JTF-6) is one such strategy. JTF-6 grew out of George Bush Sr.'s National Drug Control Strategy and is used under the Texas version of Gatekeeper, "Operation Alliance." In one such joint operation, the marines cooperated with the Border Patrol for antidrug missions on the Texas border. In 1997, an 18-year-old U.S. citizen, Ezekiel Hernandez, was shot and killed by marines under suspicious circumstances. Hernandez was riding his horse with his hunting rifle when he was shot, something he did routinely. No charges were brought against the marines, who claimed they fired in self-defense. . . .

An Ineffective Policy

A recent study reveals that Gatekeeper hasn't stemmed the flow of immigration despite the $6 billion to $9 billion spent for the operation over the last several years. According to Wayne Cornelius, director of the Center for Comparative Immigration Studies at the University of California, San Diego, Operation Gatekeeper is "a failed policy." While proponents of the policy point to the decline in arrests as a result of "deterrence," they fail to mention that detentions have increased many-fold east of San Diego, where most of the deaths occur.

Robert Martinez argues that tightening controls at certain parts of the border simply means that people try to cross in different places:

> Operation Gatekeeper is not only causing one of the worst human rights tragedies in border history, but it's totally ineffective in stopping the flow of people in crossing the border. All they are doing is moving them from San Ysidro and Otay to East County and Imperial Valley and into Arizona where the number of apprehensions has quadrupled. The same number of people are crossing—just in another area. They are touting the success of Operation Gatekeeper because they've reduced the number of apprehensions in this area, but it's very deceptive. It's a bubble effect, you squeeze here and they pop up over there.

While it is impossible to know exactly how many migrant workers cross the border in a given year, the statistics bear out what Martinez argues. INS officials claim a 30 percent apprehension rate, with a record 1,643,679 apprehensions in the year 2000. While apprehensions in San Diego have declined from 450,152 in 1994, to 151,681 in 2000, the number of apprehensions east of San Diego has increased 761 percent in El Centro, 351 percent in Arizona, and 55 percent in Texas. All told, there had been a 57 percent increase in the number of apprehensions along the Southwest border as of December 2000, giving lie to the claim that Operation Gatekeeper has been successful in curbing border crossings. Even the INS estimates that the number of people entering the U.S. illegally (55 percent of them from Mexico) each year has remained steady at about 275,000—in spite of the billions spent in the last several years to stop illegal immigration.

Anti-immigrant policies like Operation Gatekeeper are not designed to prevent immigration so much as to terrorize immigrants and to prove that something is being done to stop immigration. . . .

On the border, Gatekeeper will do nothing to stop immigration, nor is it really designed to, but it is in place to sow terror among immigrant workers. The anti-immigrant policies of which Gatekeeper is a part aim to keep immigrants divided from other workers, to keep them without rights or recourse against their abuse and exploitation, and, consequently, to inhibit their ability to form unions. . . .

Capitalism Needs Immigration Controls

Immigration policy in the U.S. has been closely related to economic swings, with greater or lesser restrictions related to the demand for labor. A migratory labor pool is essential to capitalism when economic growth produces a demand for workers that can't be satisfied by the existing workforce. But, the more "controllable" the workforce, the better. That's why immigration restrictions are never eliminated. Denying migrant workers the rights of citizenship makes them more vulnerable to arrest, deportation, and separation from their families. Migrant workers are also more likely to work the lowest-paying jobs with minimal or nonexistent safety standards in sweatshop-like garment factories, agriculture, construction, and food service. Fear of deportation deters them from organizing for better conditions. That is why the North American Free Trade Agreement opened the border to trade and investment but kept it closed for workers.

Immigration bashing is also used ideologically to try to turn U.S.–born workers against immigrant workers rather than seeing them as allies. This also explains why anti-immigrant policy has become a permanent feature under capitalism, even though the system is dependent upon workers of different countries. Such differentiation between workers on the basis of citizenship and nationality aids employers and politicians, who are more than willing to blame immigrants for the failings of the system or to call the INS in order to break a union drive. But anti-immigrant policies, such as California's Proposition 187, designed to deny immigrants basic human rights to education and social services, has also helped in turn to open the door to more far-right hatemongers like Patrick Buchanan.

The bosses and politicians have historically exploited national and cultural divisions in the U.S. to weaken working-class unity. This legacy has stifled the labor movement in this country and ensures that we live in the most unequal of the advanced industrialized countries. Immigrant bashing and harsh laws against undocumented workers, therefore, hurt not only the workers directly affected, but all workers, because, to repeat an old labor movement refrain, "An injury to one is an injury to all."

*"Many undocumented immigrants . . .
have earned access to legalization by
their hard work and demonstrably high
moral character."*

Resident Illegal Immigrants
Should Receive Amnesty

Sheila Jackson Lee

In 1986, Congress passed the Immigration Reform and Control Act, which granted amnesty to immigrants who could
prove continual residence in the United States prior to 1982.
About 2.7 million people took advantage of the law to obtain
legal status. Since the late 1980s, however, the number of illegal immigrants living in the United States has increased due to
sustained migration. Various amnesty proposals for these
more recent immigrants continue to be raised. In the following viewpoint, Sheila Jackson Lee, a democratic representative
from Texas, argues that long-term undocumented residents
who work hard and pay taxes should be given the opportunity
to earn legal status. Productive immigrants deserve to have access to educational and economic opportunities, Lee contends.

As you read, consider the following questions:
1. How many undocumented people are living and working
   in the United States, according to this viewpoint?
2. What are some of the negative consequences of denying
   legal status to undocumented residents, in the author's
   opinion?
3. According to Lee, what are the primary objectives of the
   Immigration Statement of Principles?

It needs to be said at the outset that the United States does *not* need an immigration amnesty such as the one Congress authorized in 1986. Instead of a blanket amnesty, what America needs is to allow hardworking, taxpaying individuals who have been residing in the United States for many years the opportunity to earn permanent residency status—the green card—which ultimately would lead to citizenship.

Furthermore, this opportunity should be afforded to immigrants from all nations. Many of the undocumented are from Mexico, Canada, Central and South America, the Caribbean, Asia, Africa and Europe. A fair, uniform, earned-adjustment program that benefits all immigrants regardless of their country of origin is essential. [Editor's note: As of December 2002, a new immigration amnesty had not been enacted.]

It is part of the American tradition to show compassion to immigrants. And many undocumented immigrants living in the United States have *earned* access to legalization by their hard work and demonstrably high moral character. Earned access to legalization would adjust the status of many hardworking, taxpaying immigrants, as well as students educated here who have resided in the United States for many years.

Undocumented Workers Deserve Respect

Immigrants always have made significant contributions to our country. Many, if not most, of the undocumented individuals in our country are productive and have made invaluable contributions to the U.S. economy. It would be inhumane and imprudent to tell longtime undocumented residents that they cannot become U.S. citizens. Furthermore, to perpetuate a large undocumented population is to establish a permanent second class which is subject to manipulation and criminal exploitation.

The government estimates that 6 million to 9 million undocumented people are living and working in the United States. They are a positive and essential force for growth, productivity and diversity.

Denying these people access to legalization has serious ramifications. A great number of them are children, and although they attend grammar and high school, such children have little or no chance to attend universities across our nation. Without legal status these students cannot get in-state tuition. A policy that denies education to immigrant children relegates them as a class to a life of working in low-paying, low-skilled jobs. This is as unjust as it is foolish. Allowing access to a higher education will result in great contributions to our society.

In addition, a great number of the undocumented individuals have children who are U.S. citizens. These children will grow up receiving benefits without any problems. However, these children will see how their parents are treated—as second-class. This is a situation we cannot allow.

The Immigration Statement of Principles

On Aug. 2, 2001, I, as cochairwoman of the House Democratic Caucus Immigration Task Force, and Democratic Reps. Silvestre Reyes of Texas and Luis Gutierrez of Illinois, along with House Minority Leader Richard Gephardt of Missouri and other members of Congress, unveiled a concise, comprehensive and, most importantly, an inclusive "Immigration Statement of Principles."

This statement is the fruition of the mission of the Immigration Task Force—to devise a succinct, inclusive and equitable proposal that reflects the Democratic Party's philosophy of achieving the core values of all Americans, especially family reunification, fundamental fairness and economic opportunity. In addition, the Immigration Statement of Principles stands by the people who fuel the economic engine that drives the U.S. economy.

The United States' current immigration policy has fundamental problems that must be rectified, and immigrants need and deserve redemption for what our nation's policies have forced them to go through in terms of tearing families apart and not allowing enough avenues for hardworking, taxpaying immigrants to gain earned access to legalization.

The main objectives of the Immigration Statement of Principles are family reunification, earned access to legalization, border safety and protection, an enhanced temporary-worker program and an end to unfair discrimination against legal immigrants. The Democratic mission is quite clear: We want job enhancement for immigrants and meaningful access to educational opportunities.

Family Reunification

Family reunification is essential. Our current immigration policy works to tear families apart. The current statutory ceilings for family and employment-based immigrant visas no longer are adequate and have resulted in unacceptable immigration backlogs. There are more than 1 million spouses and children of permanent residents waiting for immigrant visas that will reunite them with their families here in the United States. It is wrong for U.S. citizens and permanent residents to be forced to choose between the American Dream and a united family. We cannot deny immigrants who work hard and pay taxes the opportunity to be reunified with their families. After all, undocumented residents must pay U.S. sales, fuel and excise taxes on their purchases just like everyone else. Most undocumented workers pay payroll taxes as a condition of employment.

Adjusting the status of these longtime residents will give employers a more stable workforce and improve the wages and working conditions of all workers. Permanent residency should be available to those who are enrolled in courses in the English language or U.S. civics, demonstrate ties to their community and are admissible under our immigration laws.

A Larger Immigration Agenda

The Immigration Statement of Principles includes provisions to support the mission of the U.S. Border Patrol. We need to increase safety and security at our borders and provide Border Patrol agents with the necessary resources while ensuring safety and due-process protections to immigrants at our borders.

An enhanced temporary-worker program should be available to persons who desire to work in the United States temporarily, as well as those who choose to stay permanently. However, this program will be structured differently from past "guest-worker" programs to avoid the troubling legacy of exploitation and abuse.

While a temporary-worker program can be an effective way for immigrants to move between their home countries and the United States—and a way for recent arrivals in the United States to earn permanent status—we must recognize that a temporary-worker program can not stand alone. It must be part of a larger immigration agenda.

Extending Welcome

Dumping on immigrants, . . . contradicts the very foundations of this great country. We are a nation of immigrants. Except for Native Americans (whom we have treated even worse than illegal aliens), we are all immigrants, or descended from immigrants. Yes, legal immigrants, for the most part. But also illegals.

We should extend to today's immigrants the same welcome our ancestors received—and not just undocumented immigrants from Mexico. Those here illegally from other Latin American countries, as well as Asia and other parts of the world, deserve the same opportunity.

Bill Press, *Liberal Opinion Week*, August 6, 2001.

The Immigration Statement of Principles declares that we must end unfair discrimination against legal immigrants. This last point addresses a piece of unfinished business of the last Congress. We must restore due-process protections to permanent and other long-term residents affected by the 1996 immigration laws and restore vital public benefits.

This renewed commitment to immigration by the House Democratic Caucus advances a new immigration ethic because it is consistent and evenhanded—something immigration policy has lacked in the past. It is all-inclusive because it addresses all immigrants who are hardworking, who pay taxes and have good moral character. There simply is no reason why a restaurant worker, landscaper or meatpacker should not be able to work in the United States if a high-technology worker is able to do the same.

Immigrants contribute to our society. They share the same values that most Americans share—working hard, paying taxes and raising families. If we do not help the immigrants in our country, we will be shutting out people who want to share the values of freedom and democracy. Immigration contributes to our country's prosperity. This new immigration policy represents the hope that immigrants will reach their dream of living and working and providing a better future for their families.

This is a nation of laws, but it also is a nation of fairness, equity, humanity and democracy. And we cannot forget that we are a nation of immigrants. Our huddled masses are yearning to breathe free—to have the access and the golden door open to legalization. This is the least we can do for those who have demonstrated their commitment to our country.

4

"Amnesty sends the message that it is far easier and faster to become a U.S. citizen by immigrating illegally than it is to wait for legal approval."

Illegal Immigrants Should Not Receive Amnesty

Robert Byrd

Illegal immigrants who have worked for many years in the United States should not be granted amnesty, argues Robert Byrd in the following viewpoint. Population growth in the United States—which has been accelerated by immigration—has started to exceed the government's ability to provide adequate education, health care, and transportation to citizens. Immigrants are less likely to be educated or to have lucrative job skills than are native-born citizens, so they place even more of a burden on social services, states Byrd. Furthermore, granting legal residency to undocumented immigrants rewards people for breaking the law. Ultimately, amnesty leads to an increase in illegal immigration because it encourages others to move to the United States and ignore the processes by which one earns legal residency status or citizenship. Byrd is a Democratic senator from West Virginia. This viewpoint is excerpted from a speech he delivered to the Senate on July 23, 2001.

As you read, consider the following questions:
1. According to Byrd, what percentage of established immigrants lived in or near poverty in the year 2000?
2. What kinds of responsibilities does U.S. citizenship entail, in the author's opinion?

Robert Byrd, address to the United States Senate, July 23, 2001.

In his delightful work *Democracy in America*, Alexis de Tocqueville begins his thoughts on the origins of Anglo-Americans with these words:

> The emigrants who came at different periods to occupy the territory now covered by the American Union differed from each other in many respects; their aim was not the same, and they governed themselves on different principles. These men had, however, certain features in common, and they were all placed in an analogous situation. The tie of language is, perhaps, the strongest and the most durable that can unite mankind. All the emigrants spoke the same language; they were all children of the same people.

For generations, the United States has had the good fortune to be able to draw upon not only the talents of native-born Americans but also the talents of foreign-born citizens. Immigrants from many nations built our railroads, worked in our factories, mined our coal, made our steel, advanced our scientific and technological capabilities, and added literature, art, poetry, and music to the fabric of American life.

Of course, many of these new Americans struggled with our language and customs when they first arrived, but they learned our language, they absorbed our constitutional principles, they abided by our laws, and they contributed in a mighty way to our success as a nation.

Indeed, I believe that, particularly in the case of those who came to our shores fleeing tyranny, there has existed a unique appreciation for the freedom and opportunity available in this country, an appreciation which makes those special Americans among our most patriotic citizens.

In other words, do not go to Weirton, West Virginia, and burn the flag. No, not in Weirton. We have at least twenty-five or thirty different ethnic groups in that small steel town in the Northern Panhandle. . . .

Unprecedented Numbers

The United States today is in the midst of another immigration wave—the largest since the early 1900s. According to the latest numbers from the U.S. Census Bureau, immigrants now comprise about 10 percent of the total U.S. population. That is about 28.4 million immigrants living in the United States.

During the 1990s, an average of more than one million immigrants—legal and illegal—settled in the United States each year. Over the next 50 years, the U.S. Census Bureau projects that the U.S. population will increase from its present 284 million to more than 400 million. Immigration is projected to contribute to two-thirds of that growth.

These are unprecedented numbers. When I was born in 1917, there were about 102 million people in this country. When I graduated from high school in 1934, there were about 130 million people in this country. And today, there are 284 million people in America. This nation has never attempted to incorporate more than 28 million newcomers at one time into its society, let alone to prepare for an additional 116 million citizens over the span of the next fifty years.

Although many of the immigrants who have entered our country over the last ten years are skilled and are adjusting quickly, others have had problems. In the year 2000, according to the Center for Immigration Studies, 41.4 percent of established immigrants lived in or near poverty, compared to 28.8 percent of natives. The situation had completely reversed itself from thirty years before, when, in 1970, established immigrants were actually less likely than natives to have low incomes, with about 25.7 percent living in or near poverty compared with 35.1 percent of the native population.

The deterioration in the position of immigrants can be explained, in part, by a significant decline in the education of immigrants relative to natives and by the needs of the U.S. economy. In 1970, 7.1 percentage points separated the high school completion rate of established immigrants versus natives. By 2000, established immigrants were more than three times as likely as natives not to have completed high school, with 34.4 percent of established immigrants and 9.6 percent of natives lacking a high school diploma.

The less skilled the immigrants, the worse their employment prospects, the bigger the burden on schools, and the greater the demand for social services. The National Research Council recently estimated, in December 1999, that the net fiscal cost of immigration ranges from $11 billion to $20.2 billion per year. That is enough money to fund the operations of the State of West Virginia for about 3 to 6 to 8 years.

Population Growth and Overcrowding

As chairman of the Appropriations Committee and as a member of the Budget Committee, I well know of the extreme shortage of money to meet the needs of our own population today. Because of the 10-year tax cut that was enacted earlier in 2001, I am wrestling mightily with trying to provide enough money to educate our children, meet our health care needs, provide transportation to our population, and battle crime in our streets.

And, so, . . . I grow increasingly concerned when I read media reports about discussions within the administration to grant amnesty to three million Mexican immigrants who illegally reside in the United States.

I am very concerned that an open immigration policy only makes it more difficult to adequately meet the needs of our nation. I have found the attempt to fund critical needs for America to be among the most frustrating challenges that I have ever undertaken. I have implored this administration to take into account these critical needs.

In many school districts, overcrowding is already a major problem. As our classrooms fill to the brim, they are becoming breeding grounds for violence. Economic growth in some regions of the country, and the resulting influx of workers, has created a surge in the number of school-aged children. A less stringent immigration policy will only make this problem worse.

This country's personal and commercial highway travel continues to increase at a faster rate than highway capacity, and our highways cannot sufficiently support our current or projected travel needs. Between 1970 and 1995, passenger travel nearly doubled in the United States, and road use is expected to climb by nearly two-thirds in the next 20 years. This congestion will grow even worse as immigration traffic increases.

America Cannot Afford More People

And how will we provide for the health-care costs of these new citizens? Whether they arrive here legally or illegally, immigrants can receive federally funded emergency health-care service. As the immigrant population continues to increase, so will health-care expenditures to the federal government.

We also have an obligation to ensure the safety of the residents living in the United States—both native citizens and immigrants. Yet the Attorney General must soon release from jail and into our streets 3,400 immigrants who have been convicted of such crimes as rape, murder, and assault because their own countries will not take them back. We cannot protect our residents if our country is used as the dumping ground for the criminals of other nations.

We are struggling with ways to preserve and protect our environment. But population growth only exacerbates the increasing demands on our aging water and sewer systems, and further threatens the safety of our drinking water. Our "green spaces" are diminishing as more and more homes are being built to house our growing population. We lament the loss of and the damage to our natural resources, yet we seem unable to see the connection to our loose immigration policy.

We have a weakening economy, an increasing unemployment rate, a problem with adequately educating our people, a congested transportation infrastructure, a lack of adequate health care, and an administration that certainly is not totally unsympathetic to these needs. We cannot afford to take on more. I understand the desire to help the millions of people around the world who crave the blessings of freedom that we, as Americans, enjoy. At this time in our history, I do not know how we can possibly afford to provide for additional people who may need assistance with education, health problems, and job skills.

If we invite new masses to citizenship, we have an obligation to adequately provide for them. Yet we are presently frustrated with an inability even to provide for those who have come before and those who have been born in this country. . . .

Sending the Wrong Message

An interdepartmental group formed by the White House to suggest reforms of immigration policy is expected to include the option of granting legal residency to undocumented Mexican immigrants who have been working in the United States. The report raises the possibility of these illegal immigrants ultimately becoming citizens. Such a proposal would take this nation's immigration laws in the wrong direction.

The Immigration and Nationality Act, our primary law for regulating immigration into this country, sets out a very specific process by which immigrants may live and work in this country. To capriciously grant amnesty to three million immigrants who circumvented these processes, who have resided and worked in this country illegally, sends exactly the wrong message.

A Reward for Lawbreakers

An amnesty, whether it's called "legalization," "regulariza-tion," "earned adjustment" or any other euphemism, is still a reward for lawbreakers. In 1986, Congress passed an amnesty which ultimately benefited 2.7 million illegal aliens in what was billed as a once-in-history event. It's now clear that this claim was hollow. Today there are an estimated 7 million to 8 million illegal aliens in the United States, from countries around the world.

In the short term, such amnesties hurt mainly those prospec-tive immigrants foolish enough actually to try to obey the law. But in the long term, amnesties undermine our ability to reg-ulate immigration. In effect we are legitimizing illegal immi-gration by incorporating it into our policy structure. In other words, sneaking across the border or entering on a legal visa but failing to leave when it expires is becoming just an alter-native means of entering the United States—perhaps a little irregular, but not particularly unusual.

Tom Tancredo, *Insight*, September 3, 2001.

Such an amnesty suggests that it is possible to gain per-manent residency in the United States regardless of whether you arrived here legally or illegally.

That is the message that was sent in 1986 when President Ronald Reagan proposed a blanket amnesty to 2.7 million il-legal immigrants based largely on the mere fact that they had lived in this country at least since 1982. I supported that amnesty, after accepting the arguments of the Reagan ad-ministration that such an amnesty would reduce illegal im-migration when combined with tougher sanctions on em-ployers who hire illegal aliens.

What happened instead was that the United States sent a message to the world that illegal immigrants could gain legal status in the United States without having to go through the normal processes. Consequently, illegal immigration jumped from an estimated five million illegals in 1986 to somewhere between seven million and thirteen million illegals today; and these estimates do not even include the 2.7 million illegals who were granted amnesty in 1986.

So, . . . we should not repeat our earlier mistakes.

If amnesty is given to a class on the basis of their having broken the law, then we are rewarding breaking the law, we are rewarding a criminal act.

This is not the message that we should send to those who would consider illegally entering this country. What is worse, such an amnesty undermines our present immigration laws and suggests that these laws mean nothing if, to those who break them, the federal government simply grants amnesty with a wink and a nod.

Citizenship Should Mean Something

Millions of potential immigrants are waiting patiently for a chance to come to the United States legally. Why should illegal aliens have preference over these aliens who are waiting patiently? Amnesty sends the message that it is far easier and faster to become a U.S. citizen by immigrating illegally than it is to wait for legal approval.

Now, . . . American citizenship should mean something. It should not be something merely handed out as a means of political expediency. It should not be something that one can achieve as some kind of squatter's right, particularly when access to the soil they claim was gained illegally.

Being an American is something to be cherished, something to be revered. Citizenship in the United States brings with it certain inalienable rights. Those who would come to our country to try to establish citizenship are often enticed by the promise of those rights.

The notion that each citizen is guaranteed certain protections is powerfully alluring. But what many fail to understand is that those rights are protected only so long as Americans are willing and able to defend them. Our populace must be constantly vigilant for those things that threaten to endanger our rights, our Constitution, and our form of government. Such threats go well beyond military invasion. They include the preservation of ideals such as liberty and equality and justice, which can be so easily chipped away.

Rights and Responsibilities

In order to become citizens, most aliens are required to devote time to a study of our country and its history. They receive, at least, elementary guidance to help them appreciate the precious title of "citizen" and all that it entails. What goes all too often unspoken in this debate is that U.S. citizenship entails much more than rights. It entails responsibilities.

Our citizenry should be instilled with at least a basic understanding of the precepts that formed the foundation for this country. Lacking that, they are ill-prepared to be guardians of our future.

We Americans are justifiably proud of our history as a melting pot. If we go back far enough, we are all products of that melting pot, at least most of us. But the melting must be done in a way that ensures that these new citizens are ready to be productive, functioning Americans. We owe it not only to today's citizens but also to future citizens, including those who come to our shores expecting the opportunity for which America is so renowned. . . .

The United States today is in the midst of another immigration wave—the largest since the early 1900s. According to the latest numbers from the U.S. Census Bureau, immigrants now comprise about 10 percent of the total U.S. population. That is about 28.4 million immigrants living in the U.S.

During the 1990s, an average of more than one million immigrants—legal and illegal—settled in the United States each year. Over the next 50 years, the U.S. Census Bureau projects that the U.S. population will increase from its present 284 million to more than 400 million. Immigration is projected to contribute to two-thirds of that growth.

Periodical Bibliography

The following articles have been selected to supplement the diverse views presented in this chapter.

T. Alexander Aleinikoff   "Illegal Employers," *American Prospect*, December 4, 2000.

David Bacon   "Braceros *or* Amnesty?" *Dollars & Sense*, November/December 2001.

Ann Carr   "Deporting Resident Aliens: No Compassion, No Sense," *America*, February 27, 1999.

Simon Courtauld   "California Dreaming," *Spectator*, May 13, 2000.

Joseph A. D'Agostino   "Government Deports Only About 1% of Illegal Aliens," *Human Events*, March 2, 2001.

Paul Donnelly   "Make a Green Card the Real Payoff for Guest Workers," *Los Angeles Times*, February 12, 2001.

James R. Edwards Jr.   "Inviting Mexican Guest Workers into U.S. Would Worsen Problems," *Insight*, August 27, 2001.

Don Feder   "Amnesty Is Open Door to Illegal Aliens," *Boston Herald*, February 14, 2001.

Daniel Griswold   "Mexican Workers Come Here to Work: Let Them!" *Wall Street Journal*, October 22, 2002.

Ann Guillen   "Traveling North: A Chronicle of an Undocumented Journey," *NACLA Report on the Americas*, September/October 2001.

Wendy McElroy   "Sweatshops: Look for the INS Label," *Ideas on Liberty*, July 2000.

Roger D. McGrath   "Letter from California," *Chronicles*, October 2000.

Joseph Nevins   "How High Must Operation Gatekeeper's Death Count Go?" *Los Angeles Times*, November 19, 2000.

William G. Paul   "America's Harsh and Unjust Immigration Laws," *USA Today* (Magazine), July 2000.

Miguel Perez   "Amnesty for Immigrants Makes Sense," *Record*, February 23, 2001.

Margot Roosevelt et al.   "Illegal but Fighting for Rights," *Time*, January 22, 2001.

CHAPTER 4

How Should U.S. Immigration Policy Be Reformed?

Chapter Preface

After the terrorist attacks of September 11, 2001, the U.S. Immigration and Naturalization Service (INS) came under fire for the role that it unwittingly played in allowing foreign terrorists to enter the country. As the arm of the Justice Department charged with overseeing immigration policy, the INS had the dual responsibility of preventing unlawful immigration and of awarding citizenship to legal immigrants. Many critics maintain that the agency's lenient standards and lax enforcement policies enabled the September 11 terrorists to carry out their plans. For example, each of the nineteen hijackers had been granted visas (temporary permits to travel) from the U.S. State Department, but three of them violated the terms of their visas without attracting the attention of the INS. One of the hijackers, Hani Hanjour, was granted a student visa to study English but never attended the school to which he had been admitted. The school did not notify authorities, and Hanjour simply overstayed his visa and slipped into obscurity. "The INS is so dysfunctional it's time to scrap it," declared Republican Representative F. James Sensenbrenner, chair of the House Judiciary Committee, in 2002. He added, "[It] does not enforce the law either for those aliens who don't belong here or those aliens who legally come here and want to obey that law."

Some legislators responded to Sensenbrenner's criticisms by working to increase the effectiveness of the INS. In May 2002, the Enhanced Border Security and Visa Entry Reform Act was signed into law. This law enabled the INS and U.S. Customs to upgrade staff and technology, create counterfeit-resistant passports and visas, and share database information with other gatekeeper and law enforcement agencies. In March 2003, however, many of the service functions of the INS were subsumed into the new Department of Homeland Security as the Bureau of Citizenship and Immigration Services (BCIS). While the INS had been responsible for both border enforcement and immigration policy, the new BCIS focuses exclusively on immigration and citizenship services. Meanwhile, border enforcement is handled by the Border Patrol, which is now a separate agency in the Department of

Homeland Security. Proponents believe these changes will enable the government to manage immigration policy more efficiently.

Due to the large number of immigrants who enter and stay in the United States, policy makers are likely to propose additional changes to immigration guidelines. The authors in the following chapter debate whether and how policies affecting immigrants should be reformed.

"The United States [should] stem the tide of immigration and prevent the statistically inevitable doubling of our already-too-large population in the next 60 years."

Immigration Should Be Restricted

Dirk Chase Eldredge

In the following viewpoint, Dirk Chase Eldredge argues that America must restrict immigration to protect its environment, economy, and educational systems. The recent immigrant-fed population boom has caused overcrowding in cities, which in turn has resulted in increased pollution, power shortages, and a deteriorating quality of education. Moreover, the flood of cheap immigrant labor makes it more difficult for American workers to find jobs, and immigrants' failure to acculturate creates ethnic conflict, Eldredge maintains. He suggests that the United States impose a ten-year moratorium on all immigration to assimilate current immigrants and to plan new immigration policies. Eldredge is the author of *Crowded Land of Liberty: Solving America's Immigration Crisis.*

As you read, consider the following questions:

1. According to Eldredge, how many illegal immigrants currently live in the United States?
2. On average, how many years does it take for Mexicans to become naturalized U.S. citizens, according to the author?
3. In Eldredge's view, why should temporary farm worker programs be discontinued?

Dirk Chase Eldredge, "Q: Should Washington Stem the Tide of Both Legal and Illegal Immigration? Yes: Immigration Will Double the Population of the United States Within the Next Sixty Years," *Insight on the News*, vol. 18, March 11, 2002, pp. 40, 42–43. Copyright © 2002 by News World Communications, Inc. Reproduced by permission.

The United States will double its population in the next 60 years unless we take prompt, aggressive action. The doubling will be caused almost entirely by immigration; more than 90 percent of our population growth since 1970 has come from recent immigrants and their children born here. Only Congress and the president can prevent this calamity, but so far neither has taken preventive action. Like Nero, they are fiddling while Rome burns.

To exacerbate matters, Congress legalized nearly 3 million illegal immigrants with amnesties in 1962, 1986 and 1997. Another is being considered for the 8 million to 11 million illegals we now host. This *must* be stopped.

Dramatic Population Growth

In 1981, the Rev. Theodore Hesburgh, then-president of Notre Dame University, chaired a congressional commission to study immigration policy. The commission told President Ronald Reagan that our population was 200 million, which it labeled "already ecologically unsustainable," and recommended an immediate freeze on immigration. The commission found the root cause of our dramatic population growth to be chain immigration, a concept created by the 1965 amendments to the Immigration and Naturalization Act. The Hesburgh Commission studied chain immigration in detail, concluding that it allowed such aberrations as a family of five immigrants, if all became naturalized citizens, to grow in a relatively short period to 84 immigrants. Other studies found the multiplier to be somewhat less, but all agreed it was substantial. The study was reported more than 20 years ago, yet nothing has been done to halt population growth or reduce the dramatic effects of chain immigration. From the "ecologically unsustainable" 200 million in 1981, our population now is 281 million—and growing.

This growth has not occurred in a vacuum, but rather in the midst of the world's population exploding around us. It took from Adam and Eve to 1800 for the world to accumulate its first billion inhabitants. The pace of growth then accelerated and the world added 2 billion people in the next 160 years. Then the really frightening growth began: It took only 40 years for Earth to double its population from 3 billion in 1960 to 6 billion by the year 2000!

This accelerating rate of growth created tremendous external pressure on the United States from people in the Third World, where most of this growth occurred. They are desperate to better their lot by moving to more advanced countries such as the United States, Canada and Australia and those in Western Europe.

A Tremendous Price

Excessive immigration, both legal and illegal, resulting from the amendments of 1965, has exacted a tremendous price from the American people, paid in the coin of overcrowded schools, congested highways, deteriorating ecology and lagging infrastructure. California, for instance, would require the completion of one new school each day to keep pace with the growth of the student populations. Of course, no state is able to finance and build schools that rapidly. This shortfall causes increasingly crowded classrooms and a deteriorating quality of education. Nor is the problem limited to California. Other high-immigration states such as New York, Florida and Texas face similar demands.

Inadequate highways are another manifestation of excessive immigration. Licensed drivers in the United States have increased by 64 percent since 1970, and vehicle miles by 131 percent. Yet during that period the nation's road mileage has grown a scant 6 percent. Remember that deficit next time you are stuck in traffic.

Recently we have experienced power shortages resulting in brownouts and rolling blackouts caused by too many people using a sometimes inadequate power supply. Because in today's politically correct climate it would be considered career suicide, no political leader has admitted that excessive immigration is a major contributor to these problems.

On the ecological front, in spite of impressive progress in some areas, 40 percent of Americans live in cities where the Environmental Protection Agency deems air quality substandard. Thirty-five of our states are withdrawing groundwater faster than it's being replenished. Forty percent of our lakes and streams are unfit for fishing or swimming. Our shortage of convenient open space is a national tragedy.

Americans need tranquility more than ever, as overcrowding in our nation's population centers makes the mere absence of cell-phone babble a luxury.

Failure of Assimilation

The numbers tell why the United States suffers from immigration indigestion. During the 1960s we were absorbing 300,000 immigrants annually. Resulting from the aforementioned amendments to our immigration laws, the inflow of immigrants by the 1990s had ballooned to an average of more than 1 million per year. The dramatic change in the rate and ethnic composition of immigration brought fundamental changes to our nation, with failure of assimilation being the most profound.

The United States has a proud tradition of assimilating immigrants into the mainstream of our variegated population. Today, however, balkanization has replaced assimilation. Increasingly in America we see ethnic enclaves of recent immigrants making no effort to assimilate. Mexicans are the slowest to assimilate, perhaps because of their homeland's proximity. Alejandro Carrillo Castro, a former Mexican consul general in Chicago, says Mexicans in the United States are especially slow to naturalize, the ultimate act of assimilation. On average they take 22 years; others take seven.

Disturbing examples of balkanization are found in California and Florida, to name just two trouble spots. The Hispanic former mayor of Miami, Florida, Maurice Ferre, once declared Spanish the official language of his city and predicted that soon people either would speak Spanish or leave. Fortunately, his abrasive 1981 forecast has yet to materialize. Many Miamians would say the issue still is in doubt. Southern California's Huntington Park and Garden Grove are cities staunchly balkanized by Hispanics and Asians, respectively. Some former Garden Grove residents expressed their frustration through a bumper sticker, widely displayed in the 1990s, that read: "Will the last American out of Garden Grove please bring the flag?"

The *Houston Chronicle* reported a jarring example of nonassimilation: "At a soccer game against Mexico in February [1988], the American national team listened in frustra-

Reduce the INS Workload

The Government Accounting Office reported in May 2002 that the receipt of new applications (green cards, citizenship, temporary workers, etc.) has increased 50 percent over the past six years, while the backlog of unresolved applications has quadrupled to nearly 4 million. Few if any government agencies could be expected to handle such a crush of new work while assuming added responsibilities, even if provided with increased resources. The Immigration and Naturalization Service (INS) in particular has had a great deal of difficulty in modernizing and using additional resources. . . .

Solving the many problems with our immigration system will not be easy. There have been various plans to reorganize the INS altogether, including splitting the service and enforcement functions, into either two agencies or two separate chains of command within the current INS. But money and institutional reorganization won't be enough on their own. The best way to give the INS the breathing room it needs to put its house in order and to address homeland security concerns is to reduce its workload by reducing temporary and permanent immigration.

Steven Camarota, congressional testimony, October 12, 2001.

---

tion as a chorus of boos erupted during 'The Star-Spangled Banner.' Thousands of fans threw cups and bottles at the U.S. players, often striking them. They also attacked someone in the stands who tried to unfurl an American flag. The match didn't take place in Mexico City but in Los Angeles."

Failure of assimilation weakens America's social fabric and makes it difficult for immigrants to succeed here by participating fully in our economy. When immigration takes place at a reasonable rate, assimilation is more likely to occur. Adding to the problem of nonassimilation are more affordable airfares between the United States and immigrants' homelands, and such conveniences as reasonable long-distance telephone rates. In 1965 it cost $10.59 to call the Dominican Republic for three minutes and $15 to call India: now those rates are $1.71 and $3.66 respectively.

Stemming the Tide

Through concerned, engaged leadership, the United States can stem the tide of immigration and prevent the statistically inevitable doubling of our already-too-large population in the next 60 years. First, a 10-year moratorium for all immigration would provide time for us to assimilate and acculturate the torrent of immigrants of the last three decades. Second, it would give our underclass a chance to improve their incomes and working conditions absent the flood of cheap, immigrant labor with which they now compete for entry-level jobs. And finally, it would give us time thoughtfully to plan future immigration policies. What characteristics will we seek in future immigrants? What level of education, what skills, what ages and how many will we admit? The moratorium would provide time to develop a consensus on future immigration, supplanting today's "policy-by-pressure-group" approach.

For national-security and other reasons, our borders must be bolstered against today's silent invasion by illegal immigrants, 40 percent of whom enter with temporary visas and simply stay, melding into our society as did 13 of the Sept. 11, 2001, terrorists. Other illegals sneak across our porous borders and shorelines. There currently is no downside to breaking U.S. immigration laws. If illegal aliens are apprehended they often are simply taken back across the border and released. Hispanics at the border say: *"Es un juego."* Translation: It's a game.

We should put teeth into our laws by incarcerating apprehended illegals in military facilities made available in recent rounds of base closures: 90 days for the first offense, six months for the second and a year for the third.

It's also time to demagnetize the magnet drawing them here: jobs. By replacing the easily counterfeited Social Security card every working American now must have with one containing a biometric representation of the carrier's fingerprints, we could make it simple to determine who is legally in our country and who is eligible for welfare and unemployment. Sanctions on employers who hire illegals should be part of the new paradigm.

A free, quality education is another element of the magnet. The simultaneous states of illegal immigrant and legal student are an affront to common sense and the rule of law and should be discontinued.

"There is nothing so permanent as a temporary farm worker" is more than a clever turn of phrase; it is a truism. This should be recognized and such programs discontinued. They simply perpetuate economically unsound arrangements where U.S. farmers produce labor-intensive crops that cannot be grown and harvested profitably without cheap immigrant labor, the availability of which discourages development of automated methods. If we cannot grow such crops profitably, their production should be left to countries that can. That's how a free market, unfettered by a flow of unrealistically cheap labor, efficiently allocates its resources.

> *"Why shouldn't a person be free to cross a border, whether in search of work to sustain his life, to open a business, to tour, or simply because he wants to?"*

Immigration Should Not Be Restricted

Jacob G. Hornberger

Immigration controls interfere with individual freedom, argues Jacob G. Hornberger in the following viewpoint. The government has no moral authority to restrict one's right to cross borders to pursue work, leisure, business opportunities, or refuge. In fact, Hornberger asserts, government immigration controls often lead to immoral consequences, such as the rejection of political refugees and the abuse of undocumented workers. If Americans are to be true to their country's founding principles, they should uphold personal liberty and allow individual needs and market opportunities to determine the movement of immigrants. Hornberger is founder and president of the Future of Freedom foundation, a libertarian advocacy organization. He is coeditor of *The Case for Free Trade and Open Immigration*.

As you read, consider the following questions:

1. What is the bedrock principle underlying American society, according to Hornberger?
2. In the author's opinion, how do immigration controls restrict the freedom of American citizens?
3. What is the only permanent solution to terrorism, in Hornberger's view?

Jacob G. Hornberger, "Keep the Borders Open," *World & I*, vol. 17, January 2002, p. 44. Copyright © 2002 by *World & I*. Reproduced by permission.

In times of crisis, it is sometimes wise and constructive for people to return to first principles and to reexamine where we started as a nation, the road we've traveled, where we are today, and the direction in which we're headed. Such a reevaluation can help determine whether a nation has deviated from its original principles and, if so, whether a restoration of those principles would be in order.

It is impossible to overstate the unusual nature of American society from the time of its founding to the early part of the twentieth century. Imagine: no Social Security, Medicare, Medicaid, income tax, welfare, systems of public (i.e., government) schooling, occupational licensure, standing armies, foreign aid, foreign interventions, or foreign wars. Perhaps most unusual of all, there were virtually no federal controls on immigration into the United States.

With the tragic and costly exception of slavery, the bedrock principle underlying American society was that people should be free to live their lives any way they chose, as long as their conduct was peaceful. That is what it once meant to be free. That is what it once meant to be an American. That was the freedom that our ancestors celebrated each Fourth of July.

Beginning in the early part of the twentieth century, however, our founders' concept of freedom was gradually abandoned in favor of a totally different concept—one that defined freedom in terms of the government's taking care of people, both domestically and internationally, together with the unlimited power to tax the citizenry to pay for that service.

Whatever might be said about the relative merits of the welfare state and the regulated society, their adoption effected a revolutionary transformation in the way that the American people viewed their freedom and the role of government in their lives. Moreover, the welfare-state revolution has had enormous consequences on the daily lives of the American people.

Open and Free Immigration

Let's examine the issue of immigration, which provides a good model for comparing our ancestors' vision of freedom with what guides the American people today.

In economic terms, the concept of freedom to which the founders subscribed entailed the right to sustain one's life through labor by pursuing any occupation or business without government permission or interference. It also meant freely entering into mutually beneficial exchanges with others anywhere in the world, accumulating unlimited amounts of wealth arising from those endeavors, and freely deciding the disposition of that wealth.

The moral question is: Why shouldn't a person be free to cross a border, whether in search of work to sustain his life, to open a business, to tour, or simply because he wants to? Or to put it another way, under what moral authority does any government interfere with the exercise of these rights?

We Americans often take for granted the idea of open borders within the United States, but it is such an important gift from our founders that it deserves thoughtful reflection. Think about it: Hundreds of millions of people are free to travel on the highways through all states without ever being stopped by a border guard. It is a way of life that would have shocked most people throughout history and that still surprises many foreigners who experience it for the first time.

Most Americans like the concept of open borders within the United States, but what distinguished our ancestors is that they believed that the principles of freedom were applicable not just domestically but universally. That implied open borders not only for people traveling inside the United States but also for people traveling or moving to the United States.

One important result of this highly unusual philosophy of freedom was that through most of the nineteenth century, people all over the world, especially those who were suffering political tyranny or economic privation, always knew that there was a place they could go if they could succeed in escaping their circumstances.

Immoral Results of Restrictions

The American abandonment of open immigration in the twentieth century has had negative consequences, both morally and economically. Let's consider some examples.

Prior to and during World War II, U.S. government officials intentionally used immigration controls to prevent

German Jews from escaping the horrors of Nazi Germany by coming to America. Many of us are familiar with the infamous "voyage of the damned," in which a German ship was prohibited from landing in Miami because it carried Jewish refugees.

But how many people know that U.S officials used immigration controls to keep German Jews and eastern European Jews from coming to the United States even after the existence of the concentration camps became well known? Indeed, how many Americans know about the one million anticommunist Russians whom U.S. and British officials forcibly repatriated to the Soviet Union at the end of World War II, knowing that death or the gulag awaited them?

Margulies. © 1995 by *The New Jersey Record*. Reprinted by permission of the cartoonist.

Ancient history, you say? Consider one of the most morally reprehensible policies in the history of our nation: the forcible repatriation of Cuban refugees into communist tyranny, a practice that has been going on for many years and continues to this day.

Let me restate this for emphasis: Under the pretext of enforcing immigration laws, our government—the U.S. government—the same government that sent tens of thousands of American GIs to their deaths in foreign wars supposedly to resist communism, is now forcibly returning people to communism. That's the reason that U.S. officials attacked Cuban refugees in rafts with water cannons a few hundred yards from American shores—they wanted to capture and forcibly return these defenseless people to communist tyranny. How can this conduct be reconciled with the fundamental principles of freedom and morality on which our nation was founded?

It's also important to note that immigration controls affect not only foreigners but also the freedom of the American people, especially such fundamental rights as freedom of association, freedom of contract, and privacy. We should keep in mind Ludwig von Mises' observation that one government intervention inevitably produces perverse consequences that then lead to an ever-increasing array of new interventions. The government began with immigration quotas. Over time, we have seen the growth of an enormous government bureaucracy (the Immigration and Naturalization Service and Border Patrol) that harasses, abuses, and terrorizes large segments of the population.

We have seen the establishment of Border Patrol passport checkpoints on highways and airports inside the United States (north of the border), which inevitably discriminate against people on the basis of skin color. We have seen the criminalization of such things as transporting, housing, and hiring undocumented workers, followed by arbitary detentions on highways as well as raids on American farms and restaurants.

We have seen the construction of a fortified wall in California. This wall, built soon after the fall of the ugliest wall in history, has resulted in the deaths of immigrants entering the country through the harsh Arizona desert.

Objections and Answers

Would George Washington, Thomas Jefferson, or James Madison have constructed such a wall? We have come a long way from the vision of freedom set forth by our Founding Fathers.

Let's consider some of the common objections to open immigration.

1. *Open immigration will pollute America's culture.* Which culture is that? Boston? New York? Savannah? New Orleans? Denver? Los Angeles? I grew up on the Mexican border (on the Texas side). My culture was eating enchiladas and tacos, listening to both Mexican and American music, and speaking Tex-Mex (a combination of English and Spanish). America's culture has always been one of liberty—one in which people are free to pursue any culture they want.

2. *Immigrants will take jobs away from Americans.* Immigrants displace workers in certain sectors, but the displaced workers benefit through the acquisition of higher-paying jobs in other sectors that expand because of the influx of immigrants. It is not a coincidence that, historically, our standard of living has soared when borders have been open. Keep in mind also that traditionally immigrants are among the hardest working and most energetic people in a society, which brings positive vitality and energy.

3. *Immigrants will go on welfare.* Maybe we ought to reexamine whether it was a good idea to abandon the principles of our ancestors in that respect as well. What would be wrong with abolishing welfare for everyone, including Americans, along with the enormous taxation required to fund it? But if Americans are addicted to the government dole, there is no reason that the same thing has to happen to immigrants. Therefore, the answer to the welfare issue is not to control immigration but rather to deny immigrants the right to go on the government dole. In such a case, however, wouldn't it be fair to exempt them from the taxes used to fund the U.S. welfare state?

4. *Immigrants will bring in drugs.* Lots of people bring in drugs, including Americans returning from overseas trips. Not even the harshest police state would ever alter that fact. Why not legalize drugs and make the state leave drug users alone?

5. *There will be too many people.* Who decides the ideal number? A government board of central planners, just like in China? Wouldn't reliance on the free market to make such a determination be more consistent with our founding

principles? Immigrants go where the opportunities abound and avoid areas where they don't, just as Americans do.

6. *Open immigration will permit terrorists to enter our country.* The only permanent solution to terrorism against the United States is to address the flaws in U.S. foreign policy, which is the breeding ground for terrorism against our country. No immigration controls in the world, not even a rebuilt Berlin Wall around the United States, will succeed in preventing the entry of people who are bound and determined to kill Americans.

Reexamining Principles of Freedom

More than 200 years ago, ordinary people brought into existence the most unusual society in history. It was a society based on the fundamental moral principle that people everywhere are endowed with certain inherent rights that no government can legitimately take away.

Somewhere along the way, Americans abandoned that concept of freedom, especially in their attachment to such programs and policies as Social Security, Medicare, Medicaid, income taxation, economic regulation, public schooling, the war on drugs, the war on poverty, the war on wealth, immigration controls, foreign aid, foreign intervention, and foreign wars—none of which our founders had ever dreamed of.

The current crisis provides us with an opportunity to reexamine our founding principles, why succeeding generations of Americans abandoned them, the consequences of that abandonment, and whether it would be wise to restore the founders' moral and philosophical principles of freedom. A good place to start such a reexamination would be immigration.

"If there were no Arabic or Muslim immigrants here, . . . there would not be much of a terrorist threat at all."

The United States Must Restrict Immigration to Prevent Terrorism

Samuel Francis

In the following viewpoint, syndicated columnist Samuel Francis contends that mass immigration contributes significantly to the terrorist threat in the United States. If there were no Muslim immigrants or immigrants who harbor political or religious hostilities against America, the potential for terrorism would be minimal, argues Francis. Unfortunately, he concludes, the nation's leaders seem more concerned with their own power and wealth than they are with curbing immigration and protecting national security.

As you read, consider the following questions:

1. According to Francis, what immigration-restriction measures have been endorsed by President George W. Bush?
2. After the terrorist attack in 2001, what happened to the government's plan to grant amnesty to illegal Mexican immigrants, according to the author?
3. In Francis's view, what proves that America's ruling elites remain committed to mass immigration?

Samuel Francis, "The System Finds Immigration Control All But Impossible," *Wanderer*, November 25, 2001, p. 5. Copyright © 2001 by Creators Syndicate. Reproduced by permission.

It's been like pulling teeth, but the reality of the alien terrorist threat within the United States is finally forcing even the pro-immigration George W. Bush administration to recognize the suicidal folly of tolerating mass immigration from countries and cultures profoundly different from our own. The President himself recently uttered the first words that indicate he's starting to perceive where the real danger comes from.

Acknowledging that "never did we realize that people would take advantage of our generosity to the extent that they have," Bush ticked off a list of changes in how the country would receive—or not receive—immigrants in the future. Tighter visa security and procedures, the most popular mantra of the hour, were high on the list, but so were new regulations forbidding the entry of suspected and potential terrorists. Later that same week, Attorney General John Ashcroft unveiled a new list of 46 more groups for the list of known terrorist organizations.

Paltry Progress

This is progress, sort of. Apparently it requires immense concentration of mind and steely girding of loins for the ruling class to see that letting just about anyone who wants to come here enter the country and wander about at will is really not a good idea in itself, let alone the most effective way to deter foreign terrorists. Even with the new announcements, the President had to pause every other sentence to explain that he's really not against immigration per se.

Although we need to "tighten up the visas," Bush also insisted "that's not to say we're not going to let people come into our country; of course we are." Then again, just because some people we let into our country are evil and need to be "brought to justice," "by far the vast majority of people who have come to America are really good, decent people—people that we're proud to have here." Maybe so, but it ought to be unnecessary for the President to have to keep saying it. No doubt most of the people of Afghanistan are "really good, decent people" as well, but neither the President nor the military leaders planning the bombing campaign feel the necessity to tell us so.

Catrow. © 1997 by Copley News Service. Reprinted with permission.

As for the late and unlamented "amnesty for illegal Mexican immigrants," which dominated the news prior to September 11, 2001, it turns out that amnesty is not quite as late as some had thought. "It's not dead," says White House press secretary Ari Fleischer, but due to "other duties," drawing up the amnesty plan just "has not moved at the pace the President had hoped it would move."

Why Is There a Terrorist Threat?

What all this means is that the ruling class in general and the Bush administration in particular have not really changed their minds about immigration one iota. It's just that they have at least enough political sense to grasp that most Americans know immigration is a major reason why we have foreign terrorism at all, why we are having to worry about continuing anthrax attacks,[1] why we need to keep worrying about what immigrant terrorists are planning to do to us in the future, and why the FBI and similar agencies keep issuing warnings about imminent terrorist attacks. If there were no Arabic or Muslim immigrants here, if those here who are

---

1. In the fall of 2001, five people died after envelopes containing anthrax were mailed to several media and government addresses.

clearly sympathetic to terrorism or are clearly anti-American in their religious and political views were kicked out, there would not be much of a terrorist threat at all.

Ever since September 11, when the threats that immigration represents became obvious (as though they were not obvious before), both the dominant media and the major political leaders have been trying to keep the lid on the immigration issue. As I have noted on previous occasions, restricting constitutional liberties for Americans, from requiring national ID cards to more burdensome air travel rules to looser wiretapping and surveillance regulations, are all OK and were the first measures to be adopted, but reducing immigration and expelling anti-American immigrant loudmouths are last resorts and can be undertaken only with extended explanations and qualifications. The commitment of the American ruling class to mass immigration thus seems to be engraved in granite.

It's engraved in granite because the American ruling class no longer considers itself to be American or even wants its own nation to survive. As the late historian Christopher Lasch argued, the elites that run the United States have "revolted": against their own country, and—through mass immigration, "globalization," the erosion of national sovereignty, and free trade—are consciously managing the disintegration of their own country even as they enhance their own power and wealth. It has to make you wonder who is really more dangerous to Americans and their nation—the foreign terrorists or the domestic leaders who find it so hard to keep them outside our borders.

"Reducing the number of people we allow to reside permanently in the United States would do nothing to protect us from terrorists."

Restricting Immigration Would Not Prevent Terrorism

Daniel T. Griswold

Efforts to prevent terrorism should not include severe re-strictions on immigration, contends Daniel T. Griswold in the following viewpoint. He grants that the U.S. government has a duty to protect the nation's borders by denying entry to those with criminal or terrorist connections. How-ever, the vast majority of immigrants and potential immi-grants are law-abiding, peaceful people, and they should not be blamed for terrorism, Griswold maintains. The United States has always welcomed people from around the world who sought work, freedom, and opportunities to improve their lives. Terrorism should not put an end to this Ameri-can dream, the author concludes. Griswold is assistant di-rector of trade policy studies at the Cato Institute, a public policy research foundation.

As you read, consider the following questions:

1. According to Griswold, what actions might the government take to prevent terrorists from entering the United States?
2. What is the distinction between immigration and border control, in the author's opinion?

In the wake of the September 11, 2001, terrorist attacks on the Pentagon and the World Trade Center, the U.S. government must strengthen its efforts to stop terrorists or potential terrorists from entering the country. But those efforts should not result in a wider effort to close our borders to immigrants.

Obviously, any government has a right and a duty to "control its borders" to keep out dangerous goods and dangerous people. The U.S. federal government should implement whatever procedures are necessary to deny entry to anyone with terrorist connections, a criminal record, or any other ties that would indicate a potential to commit terrorist acts.

This will require expanding and upgrading facilities at U.S. entry points so that customs agents and immigration officials can be notified in a timely manner of persons who should not be allowed into the country. Communications must be improved between law enforcement, intelligence agencies and border patrol personnel. Computer systems must be upgraded to allow effective screening without causing intolerable delays at the border. A more effective border patrol will also require closer cooperation from Mexico and Canada to prevent potential terrorists from entering those countries first in an attempt to then slip across our long land borders into the United States.

Immigration Versus Border Control

Long-time skeptics of immigration, including Pat Buchanan and the Federation for American Immigration Reform, have tried in recent days to turn those legitimate concerns about security into a general argument against openness to immigration. But immigration and border control are two distinct issues. Border control is about who we allow to enter the country, whether on a temporary or permanent basis; immigration is about whom we allow to stay and settle permanently.

Immigrants are only a small subset of the total number of foreigners who enter the United States every year. According to the U.S. Immigration and Naturalization Service (INS), 351 million aliens were admitted through INS ports of entry in fiscal year 2000—nearly a million entries a day. That total includes individuals who make multiple entries, for example, tourists and business travelers with temporary visas, and aliens who hold border-crossing cards that allow them to commute back and forth each week from Canada and Mexico.

Isolate Terrorism, Not America

Some 30 million people enter the United States each year, almost all of them on temporary student, tourist, or business visas; about a million seek to settle here and build new lives. Restrictionists like Representative George Gekas, a Pennsylvania Republican who introduced sweeping anti-immigration legislation in June 2002, insist that letting in fewer immigrants or visitors means reducing the risk of terrorists slipping through. Such reasoning—Jeanne Butterfield, executive director of the American Immigration Lawyers Association, calls it "totally bogus"—is like banning the sale of dry beans because a couple of stones get into the pile. The point is to improve the sifting process, not to deny the U.S. the many benefits that most immigrants and visitors bring. According to the National Immigration Forum, immigrants contribute some $10 billion to the U.S. economy over and above what they cost in social services—and that doesn't include the impact of immigrant-owned businesses. Immigrants pay an estimated $133 billion in direct taxes; meanwhile, visiting students and tourists bring billions more into the economy each year.

Isolating America not only injures the economy more brutally than any number of CEO scandals can, but also dries up America's cultural richness, its identity as a land thriving on the embrace of new ideas and people. . . . America's openness has always been the core of its greatness, advocates argue, and the focus must remain on screening out those who are threats instead of on how to close the borders generally.

Alisa Solomon, *Village Voice*, July 30, 2002.

The majority of aliens who enter the United States return to their homeland after a few days, weeks, or months. Reducing the number of people we allow to reside permanently in the United States would do nothing to protect us from terrorists who do not come here to settle but to plot and commit violent acts. And closing our borders to those who come here temporarily would cause a huge economic disruption by denying entry to millions of people who come to the United States each year for lawful, peaceful (and temporary) purposes.

It would be a national shame if, in the name of security, we were to close the door to immigrants who come here to work and build a better life for themselves and their families. Like the Statue of Liberty, the World Trade Center towers stood as monuments to America's openness to immigration. Workers from more than 80 different nations lost their lives in the terrorist attacks. According to the *Washington Post*, "The hardest hit among foreign countries appears to be Britain, which is estimating about 300 deaths . . . Chile has reported about 250 people missing, Colombia nearly 200, Turkey about 130, the Philippines about 115, Israel about 113, and Canada between 45 and 70. Germany has reported 170 people unaccounted for, but expects casualties to be around 100." Those people were not the cause of terrorism but its victims.

Keep the American Dream Alive

The problem is not that we are letting too many people into the United States but that the government is not keeping out the wrong people. An analogy to trade might be helpful: We can pursue a policy of open trade, with all its economic benefits, yet still exclude goods harmful to public health and safety, such as diseased meat and fruits, explosives, child pornography, and other contraband materials. In the same way, we should keep our borders open to the free flow of people, but at the same time strengthen our ability to keep out those few who would menace the public.

Immigrants come here to realize the American dream; terrorists come to destroy it. We should not allow America's tradition of welcoming immigrants to become yet another casualty of September 11.

"Dual nationality is clearly a bad idea for America."

The U.S. Government Should Discourage Dual Citizenship

Allan C. Brownfeld

Dual citizenship—a classification that allows an individual to claim nationality or citizenship in two countries—should be discouraged in America, argues Allan C. Brownfeld in the following viewpoint. New U.S. citizens are required to take an oath of allegiance in which they vow to renounce ties to foreign nations—a vow that obviously conflicts with the concept of dual citizenship. The divided loyalties and ambivalence implicit in the concept of dual citizenship undermine the value and integrity of American citizenship, the author concludes. Brownfeld is a syndicated columnist.

As you read, consider the following questions:
1. Half of today's foreign-born population are from what region, according to Brownfeld?
2. According to the author, what is the difference between dual nationality and dual citizenship?
3. What are some examples of the problems caused by dual citizenship, in Brownfeld's view?

Allan C. Brownfeld, "Dual Nationality Threatens Integrity of U.S. Citizenship," *Washington Inquirer*, May 18, 1998, pp. 5, 7. Copyright © 1998 by the *Washington Inquirer*. Reproduced by permission.

America's foreign-born population passed the 25 million mark in 1997 and is growing at a rate four times faster than the country's population as a whole, according to the U.S. Census Bureau.

In California, one person in four is a native of a country other than the U.S. The numbers have built quickly, largely because the flow of illegal immigrants keeps growing—from about 400,000 a year in the 1970s to about 800,000 a year in the 1990s.

The big influx in recent years has been from Central and South America and the Caribbean. About half of today's foreign-born population—roughly 13 million people—were born in that region. The largest single group—7 million people—are natives of Mexico.

A Growing Trend

Of particular concern is the growing trend of "dual nationality." Under a sweeping provision of Mexico's citizenship laws adopted in March 1998, for example, any person born in Mexico or born to a Mexican national who has become a citizen elsewhere may now officially claim dual nationality. The change entitles them to Mexican passports, while keeping their American ones, and broader rights to own property and to work and invest in Mexico, though not to vote in Mexican elections—at least not yet.

Mexico is not unique in allowing dual nationality. For many years, naturalized Americans have also legally claimed nationality or even full citizenship in the countries where they were born, including Canada, Colombia, the Dominican Republic, Ireland, Poland and France.

Still, with the Mexican Embassy estimating that three million naturalized Americans will claim Mexican nationality over the next few years, the law will add by far the greatest number of dual nationals.

Bad for America

Dual nationality is clearly a bad idea for America. Theodore Roosevelt once called dual nationality a "self-evident absurdity" and some critics have likened it to polygamy.

Glenn Spencer of Voice of Citizens Together, based in California, described the new Mexican legislation as "nothing less that a large-scale movement by the Mexican Government to reverse the results of the Treaty of Guadalupe Hidalgo." Under that treaty, Mexico gave up much of what is now the Southwest after a war with the U.S. more than 150 years ago.

Naturalized Americans must take an oath of allegiance in which they swear to "absolutely and entirely renounce and abjure all allegiance and fidelity to any foreign prince, potentate, state or sovereignty." The idea of dual nationality makes a mockery of this oath.

Unfortunately, the U.S. Government has not challenged dual nationality or even dual citizenship, a stronger status that allows voting rights, of naturalized Americans or native-born ones, who can claim nationality in some countries, including Ireland, if their parents or grandparents were born there. Communities of naturalized Americans who were born in South Korea, India and China are currently pressing those governments for dual nationality rights.

Hedging Bets

The 1998 Mexican act revokes a previous law that forced anyone who became a citizen of another country to give up their Mexican nationality. The new law was passed after years of campaigning, mostly by Mexican-born Americans. Some see these efforts as a prelude to a broader push for voting rights in Mexican elections, which, if approved, would lead to the spectacle of widespread campaigning in the U.S. by Mexican politicians seeking support from millions of voters who hold dual U.S.-Mexican nationality.

John Martin, special projects director for the Federation of American Immigration Reform, says, "I think the scenario describes somebody who is in effect hedging their bets, which I think displays ambivalence about their identification with the U.S. I don't think there's any way that that can be seen as healthy for American society."

We have already seen examples of where this can lead.

In February 1998, the Mexican consul general in Los Angeles, California, Jose Angel Pescador Osuna, who spoke at a symposium tied to the 150th anniversary of the Treaty of Guadalupe Hidalgo, said, "Even though I am saying this

Loyalty Cannot Be Divided

One of the goals of the globalists is to make everyone believe we are citizens of the world, not citizens of a particular country. This concept, widely taught in the schools, tends to diminish patriotism and allegiance to one's country while promoting open borders subject only to a network of international bureaucracies.

We are also beginning to hear more frequently about "dual citizenship," but that phrase is an oxymoron. One cannot truly be a citizen of two countries because ultimately loyalty cannot be divided.

If the two countries went to war against each other, the so-called dual citizens would have to pick sides. No man can serve two masters: for either he will hate the one, and love the other; or else he will hold to the one and despise the other.

Phyllis Schlafly, *Conservative Chronicle*, May 22, 2002.

---

part serious and part joking, I think we are practicing la Reconquista in California."

Consider the night of February 15. As the U.S. soccer team left the coliseum in Los Angeles—after losing 0 to 1 to Mexico—they were pelted with water bombs, beer bottles and garbage. When the American national anthem played, it was drowned out with whistles and booing—most from Mexican-Americans. In response, the Mexican consul general suggested that the U.S. not play the Star Spangled Banner at soccer games.

In another case, Samuel Sheinbein, a native-born U.S. citizen accused of murder in Silver Spring, Maryland, fled to Israel, claiming Israeli citizenship through his father. He invoked an Israeli law that protects its citizens from being sent abroad to stand trial. His father had not even been born in Israel, but in pre-state Palestine in 1944. The U.S. is attempting to extradite Sheinbein for trial in Maryland—but as of now he remains in Israel.

A Challenge to American Citizenship

John J. Miller, author of the book *The Unmaking of Americans: How Multiculturalism Has Undermined America's Assimilation Ethic*, says,

The rise of dual nationality poses a significant challenge to the old idea that American citizenship is exclusive. . . . Since 1795, naturalization in the U.S. has required immigrants to recite an oath in which they abandon their personal foreign entanglements. . . . Many countries, however, do not consider this statement legally binding. And some naturalized Americans evidently don't take it very seriously. As many as 1,800 of them voted in Colombia's senate elections in March 1998. One U.S. citizen, Jesus R. Galvis, a city councilman in Hackensack, New Jersey, actually ran for a Colombian senate seat and proposed to represent constituents in both countries at the same time. (He lost.)

In 1996, the Dominican Republic started allowing Dominicans living abroad to vote in its elections. Ireland's law, passed in 1956, even allows the grandchildren of people born in Ireland to obtain dual citizenship.

In the case of Mexico, says Mark Krikorian of the Center for Immigration Studies, "The Mexicans may call it a dual nationality, but it's really dual citizenship lite." He equates membership in a political community to a marriage or religious affiliation. "Those kinds of relationships really ought to be exclusive," he says. "If the mystic chords of memory mean anything, then peoplehood has to mean more than the assignment of legal privileges."

The U.S. has always opposed dual citizenship. In 1958, the Supreme Court ruled that voting in a foreign election justified the revocation of citizenship, even for native-born Americans. In the 1960s, however, the Court began to rule differently. In a 1967 case, it essentially made it impossible to lose U.S. citizenship except through an explicit act of renunciation.

Now, says John Miller, it is time for Congress to act. He says, "It could impose civil or criminal sanctions on people who hold dual citizenship. Running for office or even voting in a foreign election, serving as a military officer or holding a high government position in a foreign country, or even owning more than one passport can lead to fines or prison. Congress might also want to pursue treaties in which other countries would agree to bar American citizens—or simply people living in the U.S.—from voting in their elections."

Dual nationality is a bad idea for America, and Congress has a responsibility to make its voice heard before the trend goes any further.

"Dual citizenship poses little threat to U.S. national interests."

Dual Citizenship Is Not a Threat to the United States

Peter H. Schuck and Peter J. Spiro

In the following viewpoint, Peter H. Schuck and Peter J. Spiro maintain that dual citizenship poses no threat to America and even offers several political and economic advantages. For one thing, most U.S. immigrants who retain citizenship in their countries of origin claim that their primary political allegiance is to America. The oath of U.S. citizenship highlights this political allegiance but still allows immigrants to retain emotional or economic connections to their original country, the authors point out. Consequently, while immigrants become loyal Americans, their ties to their homeland enable them to open up avenues for international trade and promote democratic values around the world. Schuck is a law professor at Yale University. Spiro teaches at Hofstra Law School.

As you read, consider the following questions:
1. Where are most of America's dual citizens originally from, according to the authors?
2. In the authors' opinion, what do Iraqi-American dual nationals likely have in common with native-born American citizens?
3. What policies can help resolve any potential problems posed by dual citizenship, in the authors' view?

Mexican & American. As of March 1998, a Mexican law enables Americans of Mexican descent to retain or regain Mexican nationality. Dual citizenship is sure to come under attack from those who fear that Americans' civic attachments are being diluted. In fact, however, dual citizenship poses little threat to U.S. national interests, and efforts to combat it would be futile and counterproductive. Indeed, there are advantages to allowing naturalizing Americans to retain their original citizenship.

Many Americans are already dual citizens. Most children whose parents are of different nationalities are born with this status. But an unprecedented increase in dual nationals is occurring as important countries of origin, including Ireland and the Dominican Republic, no longer denationalize their emigrants when they naturalize here. Mexico's law will soon create an estimated five million Mexican-American dual nationals, mostly in California. Large immigrant communities from Asian nations like South Korea and India are pressing their home governments to do the same. Meanwhile, native-born Americans of European descent are using similar legal changes in their ancestral countries to acquire the employment and other advantages that go with European Union citizenship.

Not a Threat

Is dual citizenship bad for the U.S.? Many have likened it to polygamy; Theodore Roosevelt thought it "a self-evident absurdity." In the 19th century, dual nationals of warring states might have conflicting loyalties; they were seen as potential spies and saboteurs. Dual nationality often provoked bilateral diplomatic imbroglios. The War of 1812 resulted primarily from Britain's refusal to recognize naturalization of its former subjects here. Nations sometimes mistreated their subjects, who then claimed another state's protection.

Today these concerns are negligible. Although dual nationality may occasionally complicate disputes over how nations treat individuals (though human-rights law purports to protect people of any nationality), ultimate political loyalty to the U.S.—our crucial goal—is seldom an issue. Iraqi-American dual nationals, for example, likely oppose [Iraqi leader] Saddam Hussein at least as much as other Americans do. In any event, they pose no greater threat than do legal resident aliens from Iraq, who enjoy most of the same legal rights here.

Acknowledging Interdependence

Now is a good time to re-evaluate our nation's immigration laws and policies. The American people must consider how to embrace the contributions of immigrants and in the process better our communities and nation. Our elected leaders must build an immigration system which acknowledges the increasing interdependence of our world and accounts for the migration streams which characterize the new globalization.

National Conference of Catholic Bishops, resolution on immigration, November 16, 2000.

Some critics worry that dual nationality allow foreign countries to influence our politics, a watered-down version of old "fifth-column" fears. To columnist Georgie Anne Geyer, for example, Mexico's new law seeks "to create a kind of Mexican political lobby of newly enfranchised citizens of Mexican descent whose cultural allegiance would remain in Mexico." But ethnic voting, whether by Irish-, Polish- or Taiwanese-Americans, is a venerable American tradition, even without dual citizenship. The opposite fear—that dual nationals will participate less in U.S. politics than single nationals do—is speculative.

Politically and legally, the main concern is about immigrants, not Americans who become citizens elsewhere. The Constitution prevents Congress from stripping Americans of U.S. citizenship just because they naturalize elsewhere. Since 1795, however, the law has required immigrants seeking citizenship to renounce "all allegiance and fidelity" to their old nations. But if their old nation permits its citizens to retain their original nationality, this oath lacks automatic legal effect.

Those who oppose dual nationality want to enforce the oath by requiring that it be legally effective in the country of origin. But other nations would surely not forsake their native-born nationals in the U.S., and the U.S. would then have to impose blanket naturalization ineligibility on emigrants from those nations. This would be self-defeating: We should encourage the assimilation of immigrants who want to be full Americans but who naturally retain familial, emotional and economic interests elsewhere. Such a ban would also be futile, for an immigrant who does renounce his original citizenship could always reacquire it later.

The Citizenship Oath

The oath's true significance depends on the new citizen's love for the U.S., which no law can compel but immigrants historically have deeply felt. The oath must demand his primary political loyalty to the U.S.—he must prefer America's welfare in the unlikely event of a conflict—but this political allegiance is perfectly consistent with retaining lesser loyalties to his original homeland. The oath should not encourage him to lie in his very first civic act as an American.

Simple rules and bilateral accords can resolve the other potential difficulties posed by dual citizenship. Taxes and military service are already based largely on residency, not citizenship. Conflict-of-interest laws could, for example, bar Mexican-American dual nationals from serving as U.S. ambassador to Mexico or as Mexican government officials. (The recently elected president of Latvia has given up his U.S. citizenship.)

As the risks to the U.S. of dual citizenship have diminished, the benefits have grown. Dual citizens help to expand international trade, investment and other exchanges. As naturalizing Americans assimilate our democratic values by participating as citizens here, those who retain the vote in their old countries can promote these values there, as Dominican-Americans and other dual citizens are already doing. In this way, dual nationality can become another lever in our efforts to enlarge global democracy. That is very much in our national interest.

"Birthright citizenship might seem a small issue. . . . [but] its impact is huge."

Birthright Citizenship Should Be Repealed

Bonnie Erbe

In the following viewpoint, Bonnie Erbe argues in favor of immigration restrictions, which she believes are necessary in order to accommodate the housing, employment, and medical care needs of America's most recent immigrants. In particular, she supports the proposal to eliminate birthright citizenship, which grants automatic citizenship to children born to foreign mothers in the United States. Birthright citizenship is unfair, Erbe contends, because it allows noncitizens and their American-born children to bypass the regular naturalization process that legal immigrants must adhere to. Erbe is a columnist for the *Abilene Reporter-News*.

As you read, consider the following questions:
1. How does Erbe respond to the contention that immigration restrictions are racist?
2. In California in the late 1990s, what was the annual number of foreign mothers who gave birth, according to Erbe?
3. Who is Yasser Esam Hamdi, according to the author?

Since 1965 we have witnessed not just a wave, but a tsunami of immigration, the likes of which we have never experienced in the past. Yes, there was the so-called Great Wave of immigration, whose participants sailed ashore between the late 1800s and 1925. However, the so-called Great Wave is but a tiny curl, lapping at the ocean of immigrants that has become America, especially when compared with today's tidal ingress.

Almost without anticipating the impact, Congress massively reformed immigration laws in 1965. Members abolished a system that, since 1924, had strictly enforced tight quotas on immigration, and switched instead to a laxer hemispheric and per country ceiling. In 1980, Congress again raised the number of legal entries per year, to about 270,000. Further reforms in 1986 led to today's scenario, under which we allow in more than a million legal immigrants each year (in addition to all the illegal immigrants)—enough to make our forefather's eyes bulge.

Now our population consists of 88.9 percent native-born citizens and 11.1 percent immigrants—a much higher percentage of foreign-born than during the so-called Great Wave. And this percentage, friends, is going nowhere but up. Census figures show our foreign-born population surged by 43 percent or by 8.6 million persons between 1990 and 2000—figures that also dwarf immigrant growth during the period of the so-called Great Wave.

Immigration Limits Are Not Racist

It's often called unpatriotic and worse (e.g., racist) to suggest that we begin limiting immigration. Those cries are 1) inaccurate and 2) outdated. No one who publicly advocates for immigration reform wants to place tighter quotas on Mexico or the Philippines than on the former Soviet Union or Poland (i.e., white immigrants place the same burdens on society, consume just as much housing, fuel, federal benefits, etc., as minority immigrants). And if advocates were to support race-based quotas, they should be ostracized and dismissed.

Besides, supporters of massive immigration miss one major point. The more immigrants we absorb, the tougher an existence we create for recent immigrants already here before new waves enter and compete for increasingly scarce resources. The United States faces a critical shortage of low-income housing, low-skilled jobs and low-cost medical care. New immigrants make it tougher for recent immigrants to find housing, to find jobs and to meet their basic needs—an argument those who favor floodgate immigration levels would rather ignore.

Compassionate Policies?

Of course, when the question of repealing birthright citizenship is brought up the Compassion Police immediately jump into their verbal squad cars and rush to the scene of argument. But a policy that refrains from bestowing citizenship on the children of illegals would no more be "blaming" or "punishing" innocent children than an airline would be blaming or punishing the children of hijackers by not awarding them Frequent Flier mileage for unscheduled flights to Havana.

What sort of compassionate nation says, "While you must not come here illegally, if you do somehow manage to sneak over the border, avoid arrest, survive stumbling across the desert a few days, snag some slave-wage job hidden in the shadows of our society, and then have a baby—Bingo!"?

Tom Andres, *Social Contact*, Spring 1999.

Congress and the president are in no mood to restrict immigration—somewhat odd given the current recession and the circumstances leading up to [the September 11, 2001, terrorist attacks]. Nonetheless, they could try some small, tentative limitations to see how they work. One proposal that's being touted in immigration reform circles is elimination of "birthright citizenship," under which anyone born in the United States (of a foreign mother) immediately receives citizenship.

A Legal Quirk

Birthright citizenship might seem a small issue, but California health officials were reporting in the late 1990s that 100,000 non-U.S. citizens gave birth in state hospitals each year alone. In point of fact, its impact is huge.

These children and their mothers (and other family members) automatically jump ahead of millions of other foreigners patiently waiting in line abroad for the chance to come to the United States in proper, legal fashion.

Is this quirk in American immigration law fair? No. Is it standard? No. Few other countries offer birthright citizenship. In France, children born to foreign mothers may apply for French citizenship at age 18 and only if they've resided there continuously.

Perhaps if we had similarly limited (or perish the thought, abolished) birthright citizenship, the Justice Department would not be prosecuting the case of Yasser Esam Hamdi, an al-Qaida [terrorist organization] fighter who is a U.S. citizen because he was born in Louisiana to Saudi parents on a work visa. Yet he spent most of his life in Saudi Arabia until he went off to battle Americans in Afghanistan.

But then again, that would have required a lot of foresight. Foresight and U.S. immigration policy don't seem to have much in common.

"To deny or restrict birthright citizenship would erect a new and artificial barrier between the 'accepted' citizens and the 'unaccepted' citizens of our nation."

Naturalization and Birthright Citizenship Should Be Encouraged

John S. Cummins

Immigrant naturalization and birthright citizenship should be supported, asserts John S. Cummins in the following viewpoint. The vast majority of immigrants in the United States are moral, productive individuals who are eager to become naturalized citizens. Any legislative proposals that would change the naturalization process should not be designed in a way that would make it more difficult for immigrants to become citizens, he contends. For example, birthright citizenship—which grants citizenship to all children born in the United States regardless of the status of their parents—should not be repealed. Eliminating birthright citizenship would only create an unhealthy divisiveness in American society, Cummins maintains. Cummins is the bishop of the Catholic diocese of Oakland, California.

As you read, consider the following questions:
1. What is the naturalization process designed to ensure, according to Cummins?
2. In Cummins' view, why have there been more calls for restricting immigration?

In our country's relatively brief history we have been blessed with a constant infusion of new peoples, new cultures, new hopes, new dreams, and new life through the diversity, indeed the universality of the men and women who have come to this country to make it their home.

These newcomers with their different cultures, different foods, different languages and different ways, while too often rejected at first, have all eventually been allowed to make their important contributions to an ever changing, ever new America. Decade by decade these new pieces of America have been laid side by side with the old to form the American mosaic. According to the United States Catholic Conference, it is a mosaic that the "Great Seal of the United States expresses [as] an American ideal that should inspire us in its motto: 'E Pluribus Unum'—out of many, one. This motto, recognizing national unity out of the widest diversity, reflects the reality that our nation is a nation of immigrants."

Attaining the American Dream

And yet in many ways, we are more than simply a nation of immigrants; we are a nation of immigrants who, through citizenship, seek to fully embrace all that America is and hopes to be. Today, as in decades past for many immigrants, citizenship represents the ultimate in attaining the American dream. Citizenship acknowledges the exceptional value of the immigrants and bestows fuller acceptance into American society. Through naturalization the immigrant is transformed from an "alien" into an American; no longer the stranger, but now an esteemed family member free to assert all the rights and bear all the responsibilities of American citizenship.

The naturalization process is designed to ensure only motivated and eligible immigrants attain citizenship. Immigrants pursuing citizenship must also prove their commitment and dedication to American ideals by renouncing fidelity to their country of birth and swearing allegiance to the United States and the Constitution. While standards are difficult to meet and the process often discouragingly long and arduous, immigrants continue to seek American citizenship in unprecedented numbers.

Reports of inadequate oversight and management, failure

to implement quality control measures, and the general problems that the Immigration and Naturalization Service (INS) has experienced in administering the naturalization process have received extensive Congressional and media attention. These circumstances have led some to advocate changing the standards for becoming a citizen and have set the stage for serious consideration of restrictive and, we believe, unnecessary legislation. These calls for restricting access to U.S. citizenship are particularly disturbing considering that all data continues to reveal that the overwhelming majority of immigrants and refugees in this country are of good moral character, enrich our communities, are grateful to their adopted homeland, and eager to become full-fledged citizens. Citizenship is the most precious of all benefits that the federal government can bestow on an individual; thus, the naturalization process must be performed with an integrity that ensures that only those truly eligible and meeting all the requisite criteria become naturalized. Any efforts to change the current system must be undertaken in a manner that will do more than further ensure integrity. They must also ensure fairness and efficiency. Any legislation considered in the current climate may well serve only to make the process more difficult for those seeking citizenship, render thousands ineligible for citizenship and add to the already appalling backlog—a backlog the INS has estimated at more than 1.7 million applications in November 1997.

The Importance of Birthright Citizenship

It is equally important that automatic citizenship for individuals born in the United States, regardless of their alienage or the status of their parents, be preserved in law and in the Constitution. To deny or restrict birthright citizenship would erect a new and artificial barrier between the "accepted" citizens and the "unaccepted" citizens of our nation. This would create an unhealthy and destructive divide within America and add to the number of those who feel excluded from the greater society.

As in the past, the Bishops on the National Council of Catholic Bishops Migration Committee "call on the United States Congress to recognize and support the important task

The Potential for Problems

Beyond its clear violation of the 14th Amendment, legislation to end birthright citizenship would create a new series of practical problems for citizens and government alike. Native-born Americans would have to prove their parents' citizenship in order to enjoy the rights and privileges of their own citizenship. This in turn would introduce new possibilities for racial and ethnic discrimination. A stateless class would be created—the first native-born non-citizens to grow up in America since the children of slaves before the Civil War.

Jack Kemp, online article, July 17, 1997.

of nurturing new citizens so that they may begin to play a full role in the future of this nation" and ask that INS be permitted to implement fully its new plans and procedures designed to avoid the problems of the past. The current criteria for attaining citizenship are time-tested. The standards that immigrants must meet to become citizens are high, but not so high as to be unattainable. Altering the criteria in a way that would place citizenship out of the reach of more immigrants would be detrimental to us all. Citizenship is not only of value to the immigrant, but to our nation as well. It is the traditional virtue of citizenship that renews American democracy. Therefore, it is incumbent upon our government to support programs that help immigrants to meet the requirements of citizenship and to ensure integrity, efficiency and fairness in the naturalization process that will facilitate that renewal.

The Bishops believe that citizenship plays an important role in affirming the human dignity of those who are able to take advantage of the process. Raising the rate of naturalization across ethnic groups also has an important and beneficial impact on the common good of our society. [In the words of the Catholic Bishops' Committee on Migration] "By becoming citizens, immigrants reinforce the equities that they have built in this country and become full partners in the course and life of our nation." And thus the marked increase in immigrants seeking citizenship must be viewed in a positive light, because it surely tells us that these newcomers have bound their lives and their futures inextricably to that of our nation's.

We must continually remind ourselves that all newcomers aspire to become an integral part of their new homeland. All wish to be truly American, conveying enduring values to our families, our churches, our country. Any attempt to reject or discourage their presence or participation, overtly or subtly, is unacceptable. It would be particularly egregious if we were to close the door of full membership in American society to those born within our borders, or to deserving immigrants and refugees who are dedicated to the American way of life. We must look at the immigrants in our midst, not as strangers, but as new Americans in the making, helping us to forge a new and better America.

Periodical Bibliography

The following articles have been selected to supplement the diverse views presented in this chapter.

Nick Anderson	"Push to Ease Immigration Rules Is Finished for Now," *Los Angeles Times*, October 15, 2002.
Linda Chavez	"Don't Seal the Borders," *Wall Street Journal*, November 21, 2001.
Amitai Etzioni	"Rights and Responsibilities, 2001," *Responsive Community*, Winter 2001/2002.
Arthur Jones	"Immigrants Draw Harsh Terms for Simple Mistakes," *National Catholic Reporter*, September 29, 2000.
Donald Kerwin	"Looking for Asylum, Suffering in Detention," *Human Rights*, Winter 2001.
James M. Lindsay and Gregory Michealidis	"A Timid Silence on America's Immigration Challenge," *San Diego Union-Tribune*, January 5, 2001.
Robert McChesney	"Immigration and Terrorism: The Issues Have Become Blurred and Entangled," *America*, October 29, 2001.
John J. Miller	"Border Lines: What to Do About Immigration After 9/11," *National Review*, October 15, 2001.
Chitra Ragavan, Douglas Pasternak, and Edward T. Pound	"Coming to America," *U.S. News & World Report*, February 18, 2002.
Robert J. Samuelson	"The Limits of Immigration," *Newsweek*, July 24, 2000.
Abby Scher	"Access Denied: Immigrants and Health Care," *Dollars & Sense*, May/June 2001.
Gary Snyder	"Erasing Borders: Human Flow on Turtle Island," *Whole Earth*, Summer 2002.
Alisa Solomon	"Protecting the Homeland: Ten Ways to Keep America Safer Without Trampling on Immigrants," *Village Voice*, July 30, 2002.
Dan Stein	"Strip Terrorists of Their Legal Cover," *Los Angeles Times*, January 22, 2002.
James H. Walsh	"Three Ways to Stop Foreign Terrorists," *Social Contract*, Winter 2002.

For Further Discussion

Chapter 1

1. List some of the examples Thomas L. Nichols gives of the benefits of immigration. What examples does Garrett Davis provide of the drawbacks of immigration? Whose use of examples do you find more convincing? Explain your answer.

2. According to Peter Roberts, in what ways do immigrants adversely affect America's economy? In Frank Julian Warne's opinion, how has immigration benefited the economy? Do you think Warner effectively counters Roberts's argument? Why or why not?

3. John F. Kennedy, a third-generation American, maintains that immigration should not be limited by a national origins quota system. Marion Moncure Duncan, whose ancestors came to America before the Revolutionary War, asserts that such quotas are appropriate and necessary. In your opinion, how might the authors' family backgrounds affect the stances they take in their viewpoints? Do you find any actual evidence of such influence in the viewpoints?

Chapter 2

1. Lawrence Auster writes that the increase in immigration from non-Western nations creates ethnic conflict and threatens American cultural values. Ben Wattenberg asserts that immigrants actually strengthen America by increasing its population and by exporting Western values to relatives abroad. Whose viewpoint do you agree with? Why?

2. George J. Borjas argues that massive immigration is straining the nation's economy because immigrants often apply for welfare and compete with low-skilled native-born workers for jobs. Joel Kotkin maintains that growing populations of immigrants are helping the economy by providing a market for consumer goods and by opening up small businesses. What evidence does each author present to support his conclusion? Whose argument is more persuasive? Explain.

Chapter 3

1. Do you agree with Justin Akers that Operation Gatekeeper and similar Border Patrol policies are responsible for the deaths of hundreds of undocumented migrants? Should any of the blame be placed on the immigrants themselves? Why or why not? Use evidence from the viewpoints in defending your answer.

2. Sheila Jackson Lee asserts that "tax-paying, law-abiding" un-documented workers should be granted amnesty so that they can become permanent legal residents of the United States. Why does Robert Byrd object to this proposal? Does his viewpoint effectively refute Lee's arguments? Explain.

Chapter 4

1. Dirk Chase Eldredge argues that immigration must be restricted because it is adversely affecting America's economy, environment, and culture. Jacob G. Hornberger maintains that immigration restrictions give the government too much control over individual needs and freedoms. Eldredge is the author of the book *Crowded Land of Liberty: Solving America's Immigration Crisis*. Hornberger is president of the Future of Freedom Foundation, a libertarian group that advocates a limited role for government and the protection of individual liberties. How does knowing the backgrounds of these authors affect your assessment of their arguments? Explain.

2. The viewpoints in this chapter include several recommendations for reforming U.S. immigration policy. Consider each recommendation and then list arguments for and against each one. Note whether the arguments are based on facts, values, emotions, or other considerations. If you believe a recommendation should not be considered at all, explain why.

Organizations to Contact

The editors have compiled the following list of organizations concerned with the issues debated in this book. The descriptions are derived from materials provided by the organizations. All have publications or information available for interested readers. The list was compiled on the date of publication of the present volume; the information provided here may change. Be aware that many organizations take several weeks or longer to respond to inquiries, so allow as much time as possible.

American-Arab Anti-Discrimination Committee (ADC)
4201 Connecticut Ave., Washington, DC 20008
(202) 244-2990 • fax: (202) 244-3196
e-mail: adc@adc.org • website: www.adc.org

ADC is a nonsectarian, nonpartisan civil rights organization dedicated to combating discrimination against people of Arab heritage and promoting intercultural awareness. It works to protect Arab American rights through a national network of chapters. The committee publishes the newsletter *ADC Times* ten times a year as well as an annual special report summarizing incidents of hate crimes, discrimination, and defamation against Arab Americans.

American Friends Service Committee (AFSC)
1501 Cherry St., Philadelphia, PA 19102
(215) 241-7000 • fax: (215) 241-7275
e-mail: afscinfo@afsc.org • website: www.afsc.org

The AFSC is a Quaker organization that attempts to relieve human suffering and find new approaches to world peace and social justice through nonviolence. It lobbies against what it believes to be unfair immigration laws, especially sanctions criminalizing the employment of illegal immigrants. It has published *Sealing Our Borders: The Human Toll*, a report documenting human rights violations committed by law enforcement agents against immigrants.

American Immigration Control Foundation
PO Box 525, Monterey, VA 24465
(540) 468-2022 • fax: (540) 468-2024
e-mail: aicfndn@cfw.com • website: www.aicfoundation.com

The AIC Foundation is an independent research and education organization that believes massive immigration, especially illegal immigration, is harming America. It calls for an end to illegal immigration and for stricter controls on legal immigration. The foundation publishes several pamphlets, monographs, and booklets, including Joseph L. Daleiden's *Selling Our Birthright* and Lawrence Auster's *Huddled Cliches.*

American Immigration Lawyers Association (AILA)
918 F Street NW, Washington, DC 20004
(202) 216-2400 • fax: (202) 783-7853
website: www.aila.org

AILA is a professional association of lawyers who work in the field of immigration and nationality law. It publishes the *AILA Immigration Journal* and compiles and distributes a continuously updated bibliography of government and private documents on immigration laws and regulations.

Americans for Immigration Control (AIC)
PO Box 738, Monterey, VA 24465
(540) 468-2023 • fax: (540) 468-2026
e-mail: aic@immigrationcontrol.com
website: www.immigrationcontrol.com

AIC is a lobbying organization that works to influence Congress to adopt legal reforms that would reduce U.S. immigration. It calls for increased funding for the U.S. Border Patrol and the deployment of military forces to prevent illegal immigration. It also supports sanctions against employers who hire illegal immigrants and opposes amnesty for such immigrants. AIC offers articles and brochures that state its position on immigration.

Bureau of Citizenship and Immigration Services
U.S. Department of Homeland Security
website: www.bcis.gov

The Bureau, an agency of the Department of Homeland Security, is charged with enforcing immigration laws and regulations, as well as administering immigrant-related services, including the granting of asylum and refugee status. It produces numerous reports and evaluations on selected programs. Statistics and information on immigration and immigration laws as well as congressional testimony, census reports, and other materials are available on its website.

California Coalition for Immigration Reform (CCIR)
PO Box 2744-117, Huntington Beach, CA 92649
(714) 665-2500 • fax: (714) 846-9682
website: www.ccir.net

CCIR is a grassroots volunteer organization representing Americans concerned with illegal immigration. It seeks to educate and inform the public and to effectively ensure enforcement of the nation's immigration laws. CCIR publishes alerts, bulletins, video-tapes, and audiotapes.

Center for Immigrants Rights (CIR)
48 St. Marks Place, 4th Floor, New York, NY 10003
(212) 505-6890

The center offers immigrants information concerning their rights. It provides legal support, advocacy, and assistance to immigrants and strives to influence immigration policy. The center publishes fact sheets on immigrant rights and immigration law and the quarterly newsletter *CIR Report.*

Center for Immigration Studies
1522 K St. NW, Suite 820, Washington, DC 20005-1202
(202) 466-8185 • fax: (202) 466-8076
e-mail: center@cis.org • website: www.cis.org

The center studies the effects of immigration on the economic, social, demographic, and environmental conditions in the United States. It believes that the large number of recent immigrants has become a burden on America and favors reforming immigration laws to make them more consistent with U.S. interests. The center publishes editorials, reports, and position papers.

Council on American-Islamic Relations (CAIR)
453 New Jersey Ave. SE, Washington, DC 20003
(202) 488-8787 • fax: (202) 488-0833
e-mail: cair@cair-net.org • website: www.cair-net.org

CAIR is a nonprofit membership organization that presents an Islamic perspective on public policy issues and challenges the misrepresentation of Islam and Muslims. It publishes the quarterly newsletter *Faith in Action* and other various publications on Muslims in the United States. Its website includes statements condemning both the September 11, 2001, terrorist attacks and discrimination against Muslims.

El Rescate
1313 West 8th Street, Suite 200, Los Angeles, CA 90017
(213) 387-3284 • fax: (213) 387-9189
website: www.elrescate.org

E1 Rescate provides free legal and social services to Central American refugees. It is involved in federal litigation to uphold the constitutional rights of refugees and illegal immigrants. It compiles and distributes articles and information and publishes the newsletter *El Rescate.*

Federation for American Immigration Reform (FAIR)
1666 Connecticut Ave. NW, Washington, DC 20009
(202) 328-7004 • fax: (202) 387-3447
e-mail: info@fairus.org • website: www.fairus.org
FAIR works to stop illegal immigration and to limit legal immigration. It believes that the growing flood of immigrants into the United States causes higher unemployment and taxes social services. FAIR has published many reports and position papers, including *Running in Place, Immigration and U.S. Energy Usage*, and *Invitation to Terror: How Our Immigration System Still Leaves America at Risk*.

The Heritage Foundation
214 Massachusetts Ave. NE, Washington, DC 20002-4999
(202) 546-4400 • fax: (202) 546-8328
e-mail: info@heritage.org • website: www.heritage.org
The foundation is a conservative public policy research institute. It has published articles pertaining to immigration in its Backgrounder series and in its quarterly journal, *Policy Review*.

National Alliance Against Racist and Political Repression (NAARPR)
11325 S. Wabash Ave., Suite 105, Chicago, IL 60605
(312) 939-2750 • fax: (773) 929-2613
e-mail: info@naarpr.org • website: www.naarpr.org
NAARPR is a coalition of political, labor, church, civic, student, and community organizations that oppose the many forms of human rights repression in the United States. It seeks to end the harassment and deportation of illegal immigrant workers. The alliance publishes pamphlets and a quarterly newsletter, *The Organizer*.

National Council of La Raza (NCLR)
1111 19th St. NW, Suite 1000, Washington, DC 20036
(202) 785-1670
website: www.nclr.org
NCLR is a national organization that seeks to improve opportunities for Americans of Hispanic descent. It conducts research on many issues, including immigration, and opposes restrictive immigration laws. The council publishes and distributes congressional testimony and policy reports, including *Unfinished Business: The Immigration Control and Reform Act of 1986* and *Unlocking the Golden Door: Hispanics and the Citizenship Process*.

National Immigration Forum
220 I St. NE, Suite 220, Washington, DC 20002-4362
(202) 544-0004 • fax: (202) 544-1905
website: www.immigrationforum.org

The forum believes that immigration strengthens America and that welfare benefits do not attract illegal immigrants. It supports effective measures aimed at curbing illegal immigration and promotes programs and polices that help refugees and immigrants assimilate into American society. The forum publishes the annual *Immigration Policy Handbook* as well as editorials, press releases, and fact sheets.

National Network for Immigrant and Refugee Rights
210 Eighth St., Suite 307, Oakland, CA 94607
(510) 465-1984 • fax: (510) 465-1885
e-mail: nnirr@nnirr.org • website: www.nnirr.org

The network includes community, church, labor, and legal groups committed to the cause of equal rights for all immigrants. These groups work to end discrimination and unfair treatment of illegal immigrants and refugees. The network aims to strengthen and coordinate educational efforts among immigration advocates nationwide. It publishes a monthly newsletter, *Network News*, and reports, including *From the Borderline to the Colorline: A Report on Anti-Immigrant Racism in the United States*.

Negative Population Growth, Inc. (NPG)
1717 Massachusetts Ave. NW, Suite 101, Washington, DC 20036
(202) 667-8950 • fax: (202) 667-8953
e-mail: npg@npg.org • website: www.npg.org

NPG believes that world population must be reduced and that the United States is already overpopulated. It calls for an end to illegal immigration and an annual cap on legal immigration of 200,000 people. This would achieve "zero net migration" because 200,000 people exit the country each year, according to NPG. NPG frequently publishes position papers on population and immigration in its *NPG Forum*. It also publishes a quarterly newsletter, *Population and Resource Outlook*.

The Rockford Institute
928 N. Main St., Rockford, IL 61103
(815) 964-5053
e-mail: info@rockfordinstitute.org
website: www.chroniclesmagazine.org

The institute is a conservative research center that studies capitalism, religion, and liberty. It has published numerous articles questioning immigration and legalization policies in its monthly magazine, *Chronicles*.

Bibliography of Books

Rodolfo Acuna — *Sometimes There Is No Other Side: Chicanos and the Myth of Equality.* Notre Dame, IN: University of Notre Dame Press, 1998.

Dale Anderson — *Arriving at Ellis Island.* Milwaukee, WI: Gareth Stevens, Inc., 2002.

Nicholas Blake and Raza Husain — *Immigration, Asylum, and Human Rights.* New York: Oxford University Press, 2002.

James M. Blume — *Illegal Aliens: Changes in the Process of Denying Aliens Entry into the United States.* Collingdale, PA: DIANE, 2000.

George J. Borjas — *Heaven's Door: Immigration Policy and the American Economy.* Princeton, NJ: Princeton University Press, 1999.

Mary Elizabeth Brown — *Shapers of the Great Debate on Immigration: A Biographical Dictionary.* Westport, CT: Greenwood, 1999.

Farai Chideya — *The Color of Our Future: Race in the 21st Century.* New York: Quill, 2000.

Roger Daniels and Otis L. Graham — *Debating American Immigration, 1882–Present.* Lanham, MD: Rowman & Littlefield, 2001.

Debra L. Delaet — *U.S. Immigration Policy in an Age of Rights.* Westport, CT: Praeger, 2000.

Michael A.E. Dummett — *On Immigration and Refugees.* New York: Routledge, 2001.

David W. Haines and Karen E. Rosenblum — *Illegal Immigration in America: A Reference Handbook.* Westport, CT: Greenwood, 1999.

Victor Davis Hanson — *Mexifornia: A State of Becoming.* San Francisco, CA: Encounter Books, 2003.

Helene Hayes — *U.S. Immigration Policy and the Undocumented: Ambivalent Laws, Furtive Lies.* Westport, CT: Praeger, 2001.

Arthur C. Helton — *The Price of Indifference: Refugees and Humanitarian Action in the New Century.* New York: Oxford University Press, 2002.

Barbara Brooks Kimmel and Alan M. Lubiner — *Immigration Made Simple: An Easy to Read Guide to the U.S. Immigration Process.* Chester, NJ: Next Decade, Inc., 2002.

David Kyle and Rey Koslowski, eds. — *Global Human Smuggling: Comparative Perspectives.* Baltimore, MD: Johns Hopkins University Press, 2001.

Ruben Martinez   *Crossing Over: A Mexican Family on the Migrant Trail.* New York: Picador, 2002.

Joseph Nevins and Mike Davis   *Operation Gatekeeper: The Rise of the 'Illegal Alien' and Remaking of U.S.-Mexico Boundary.* New York: Routledge, 2002.

Mei Ling Rein et al., eds.   *Immigration and Illegal Aliens: Burden or Blessing?* Wylie, TX: Information Plus, 1999.

Belinda I. Reyes, Hans P. Johnson, and Richard Van Swearingen   *Holding the Line? The Effect of the Recent Border Build-Up on Unauthorized Immigration.* San Francisco, CA: Public Policy Institute of California, 2002.

Peter D. Salins   *Assimilation, American Style.* New York: Basic Books, 2000.

Saskia Sassen   *Guests and Aliens.* New York: Norton, 2000.

Joseph Wayne Smith, Graham Lyons, and Evonne Moore   *Global Meltdown: Immigration, Multiculturalism, and National Breakdown in the New World Disorder.* Westport, CT: Praeger, 1998.

Michael Teitelbaum   *Threatened Peoples, Threatened Borders: World Migration and U.S. Policy.* New York: Norton, 2000.

Julie R. Watts   *Immigration Policy and the Challenge of Globalization: Unions and Employers in Unlikely Alliance.* Ithaca, NY: Cornell University Press, 2002.

Michael Welch   *Retained: Immigration Laws and the Expanding INS Jail Complex.* Philadelphia, PA: Temple University Press, 2002.

Index